BARBARIANS
AGAINST ROME

ROME'S CELTIC, GERMANIC, SPANISH AND GALLIC ENEMIES

BARBARIANS
AGAINST ROME

ROME'S CELTIC, GERMANIC, SPANISH AND GALLIC ENEMIES

TEXT BY
PETER WILCOX   RAFAEL TREVIÑO

First published in Great Britain in 2000 by Osprey Publishing,
Elms Court, Chapel Way, Botley, Oxford OX2 9LP, United Kingdom
Email: info@ospreypublishing.com

Previously published as Men-At-Arms 129 *Rome's Enemies 1: Germanics and Dacians*
Men-at-Arms 158 *Rome's Enemies 2: Gallic and British Celts* and
Men-at-Arms 180 *Rome's Enemies 4: Spanish Armies*

ISBN 1 84176 154 0

Editor: Chris Wheatley

Filmset in Singapore by Pica Ltd
Printed in China through World Print Ltd

00 01 02 03 04 10 9 8 7 6 5 4 3 2 1

FOR A CATALOGUE OF ALL TITLES PUBLISHED BY
OSPREY MILITARY, AUTOMOTIVE AND AVIATION PLEASE WRITE TO:

The Marketing Manager, Osprey Direct UK, PO Box 140,
Wellingborough, Northants NN8 4ZA, UK
Tel: +44 (0) 1933 443863, Fax: +44 (0) 1933 443840
Email: info@ospreydirect.co.uk

The Marketing Manager, Osprey Direct-USA, P.O. Box 130,
Sterling Heights, MI 48311-0130, USA
Tel: 810 795 2763, Fax: 810 795 4266
Email: info@ospreydirectusa.com

VISIT OSPREY AT:
www.ospreypublishing.com

PAGE 2 Reconstructed drawing of a Saxon warrior, probably an
ex-Roman soldier, from Lower Saxony (based on a 4th century grave
at Liebenau.

CONTENTS

Chronology

See Glossary of terms and names on page 38.

3000 B.C. Indo-Europeans spread into north-west Europe, where they settle among earlier populations of Neolithic farmers and Old Stone-Age hunters.

2000 B.C. Celto-Ligurian tribes are in control of large areas of central and western Europe. Represented by the 'Bell-Beaker Folk', they begin moving into the British Isles. Other Indo-Europeans move east, where the Thracians and Iranians form two large groups. The Balts and Slavs occupy most of what is now Germany. Illyrian tribes occupy an area of southern Europe between the Italian peninsula and Greece. (Italic Indo-Europeans had moved into their peninsula, and warlike Greek tribes into the Mediterranean area, from the Danube region.)

The Teutons of this period are in possession of most of the Scandinavian peninsula, where a racially distinct Germanic Nordic has developed from a mixture of invading Indo-European Nordics and Old Stone-Age survivors. Indo-European tribes now possess most of Europe at the expense of the earlier stock who are now either pushed into the more inaccessible parts of the continent, or become the lower strata of society, the untouchables of Europe.

Germans, from Trajan's Column, dedicated in 113 A.D.; their impressive physique is clearly illustrated. One sports the Suebian hair-knot. Two cloak styles are evident: one is large, folded double, with a thick fringe of tassels, while the other (top right) is a circular type with a diagonal head-opening.

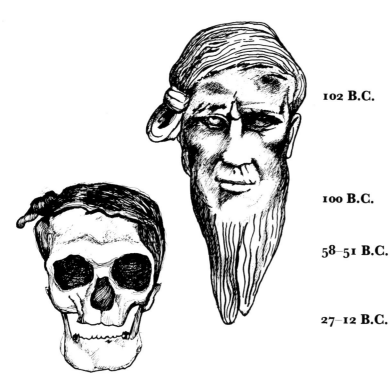

The skull of an old man, 1st century A.D., found at Eckennford, Schleswig-Holstein; the reddish blonde hair is combed and twisted into a neat Suebian knot. Compare this with the carved head of a German chieftain, possibly of one of the Danubian tribes, from the tomb of A. Julius Pompilius, one of Marcus Aurelius's generals, 175 A.D. (National Museum, Terme)

600 B.C. The continental Celts begin the Halstatt phase of their magnificent Iron Age culture; at about this time they over-run central Spain.

400 B.C. The second phase of Celtic Iron Age culture evolves; known as the La Tène, it represents the flowering of Celtic abstract art, seen, *inter alia*, in the decoration of weapons. Halstatt Celts move into Britain.

La Tène Celts cross the Alps and take control of northern Italy. Etruscan colonies in the Po valley are obliterated, and Rome is sacked during a protracted Celtic raid down the peninsula.

350 B.C. Rome defeats the Celts in Italy.

300 B.C. Rome gains full control of Italy.

115 B.C. Celtic tribes from the middle Danube area, the Cimbri and Teutones invade Gaul; during the extensive raid they attract the Ambrones—another Celtic tribe—to their ranks, and destroy five Roman armies sent against them before turning towards Italy.

102 B.C. The Cimbri, Teutones and Ambrones are annihilated by the new model Roman army, which had been created, trained and was now led to victory by Marius, a General of obscure background.

100 B.C. The Goths cross the Baltic from the Scandinavian peninsula to northern Germany.

58–51 B.C. Julius Caesar conquers most of the Celtic tribes of Gaul and reportedly repulses an attempted invasion by trans-Rhenian tribes.

27–12 B.C. Roman forces advance in central and eastern Europe, to the Danube; the river thus forms, for most of its length, the northern frontier of the Empire. The expansion of the Frontier to the Elbe in the north is called off after the disaster in the Teutoburg Forest. At about this time Augustus creates a standing army of 25 legions.

A.D. 9. The garrison of northern Germany, consisting of the XVII, XVIII and XIX Legions are wiped out in an ambush in the Teutoburg Forest. These three legions never again appeared on the army list. The Rhine-Danube nexus now marks the northern limits of the Roman Empire.

A.D. 43. Roman forces invade Britain, speedily overrunning a third of the country, from the southern coast.

A.D. 69–79. The angle formed by the Rhine and Danube is rounded off. Roman occupation of the British lowlands is carried up to the highlands. A further two legions are lost during a revolt of auxiliaries on the Rhine.

A.D. 81. Several campaigns are mounted by the Roman army on the Danube, particularly against the Thracian kingdom of Dacia.

A.D. 101. The Emperor Trajan begins a massive invasion of Dacia; in two campaigns the Romans break Dacian resistance. The conquest creates a trans-Danubian salient of the Empire. Roman forces on the Danube are reinforced by four legions; Rhine legions are reduced by three.

A.D. 150. Eastern German tribes begin drifting south; some of them enter into permanent federation.

A.D. 181. A massive barbarian assault on the Danube provinces led by the Marcomanni and Quadi triggers off a prolonged series of savagely fought campaigns during the reign of the philosopher soldier Marcus Aurelius.

A.D. 251. The Goths invade the Balkans and Anatolia; the Emperor Decius (Hostilianus) is killed.

A.D. 256. Frankish and Alemannic war bands overrun Gaul and invade Spain and Italy.

A.D. 275. Roman forces abandon both the Dacian salient and the Rhine-Danube angle in the face of increasing pressure along the northern frontier; the Gepids and Goths move into Dacia; the Alemanni occupy the Rhine-Danube angle and Burgundian tribes the middle Rhine area.

A.D. 280. The Goths, led by their king Ermanarich, spread into a large area of Eurasia and north to the Baltic. 'Anglo-Saxon' raids increase on the east coast of Britain and northern coast of Gaul.

A.D. 358. The Alemanni and Franks are defeated by the Emperor Julian in Gaul; some Franks remain in northwest Gaul as armed peasant marchmen (foederates), allies of Rome.

A.D. 360. The Ostrogoths come into contact with westward-moving Huns, a Turco-Mongoloid people.

A.D. 372. The Huns of the Volga attack the advancing Goths, who are overwhelmed by the nomadic hordes. The Huns are able to push into Europe, where they settle as the overlords of Slavonic peasants and Gepids on the Hungarian plains.

A.D. 375. The Goths and Asding Vandals apply for sanctuary within the Empire. They are settled along the Danube, where they suffer many indignities at the hands of Roman merchants and officials.

A.D. 378. The Visigoths are in revolt against Rome.

A.D. 379. The Emperor of the East is killed, his army annihilated at Adrianople by the largely cavalry army of the Goths.

A.D. 380. Germans, Sarmatians and Huns are taken into Imperial service; as a consequence, barbarian leaders begin to play an increasingly active rôle in the life of the Empire.

Reconstruction of cut of woollen twill tunic and trousers from Angeln, Denmark, dated to the 1st century B.C.

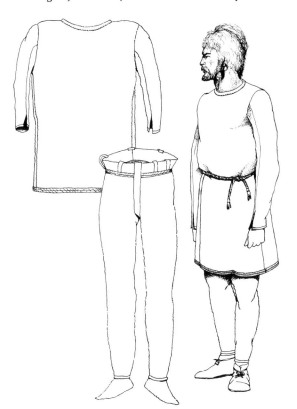

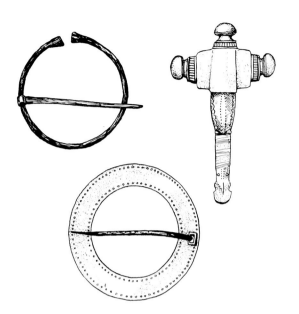

German cloak brooches.

A.D. 402. The Goths invade Italy, where they suffer defeat at the hands of the Romano-Vandal General Stilicho.

A.D. 405. Stilicho crushes a mixed army of Ostrogoths, Quadi and Asding Vandals with an army raised from the frontier forces of the Rhine, leaving this sector dangerously weakened.

A.D. 406. A coalition of Asding Vandals, Siling Vandals, Marcomanni, Quadi and a clan of Sarmatian Alans cross the frozen Rhine near Mainz into Gaul.

A.D. 407. Britain is denuded of the Roman garrison, which crosses the Channel in force in a sham effort to pacify the German invaders of Gaul. In fact they declare one of their number to be Emperor and seek recognition from the Franks, Burgundians and Alemanni who have occupied the left bank of the Rhine.

A.D. 409. The great barbarian coalition of Vandals, Suevi and Sarmatians which had ravaged Gaul for three years crosses the Pyrenees into Spain.

A.D. 410. Britain fragments under the local control of petty Romano-Celtic magnates. The Visigoths, led by Alaric, sack Rome.

A.D. 412. The Visigoths, in Imperial service, enter Gaul and depose yet another Imperial usurper.

A.D. 414. The Visigoths cross into Spain, where they exterminate the settled Siling Vandals and Sarmatian Alans (416). The Asding Vandals, Marcomanni and Quadi are spared, by Roman intervention, in order to prevent the increase of Visigothic power. As the reward for their exertions the Visigoths are invited by Roman authorities to settle in a large area of south-west Gaul.

A.D. 428. North Africa is invaded by the Asding Vandals; they build a pirate fleet and hold the Roman corn supply to ransom.

A.D. 433. Attila the Hun is born.

A.D. 436. The Huns drive deep into Germanic territory; many tribes become Hunnish vassals.

A.D. 449. German tribes begin the permanent settlement of Britain.

A.D. 451. Attila leads the Huns and their German vassals into Gaul; they are met and driven back by Roman troops, Burgundians, Salian Franks and Visigoths at the Campus Mauriacus. The Huns withdraw to Hungary.

A.D. 452. Attila invades Italy, but the Huns are bribed by Roman authorities to retire.

A.D. 453. Attila dies. The Vandals sack Rome.

A.D. 454. German vassals of the Huns overthrow their masters at the battle of Nedao.

A.D. 469–78. The Visigoths conquer most of Spain. The German general Odoacer becomes king of Italy and is recognised by the Eastern Roman Empire.

A.D. 493. Theodoric, king of the Ostrogoths, becomes Regent of Italy.

A.D. 507. The Franks expand into a large area of Gaul led by their king, Clovis.

A.D. 526. Theodoric dies.

A.D. 528. After defeating the Gepids the Lombards, helped by Avar nomads, invade Italy and make a permanent settlement in the north.

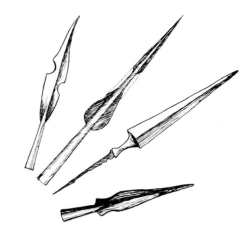

Celtic iron spearheads of the La Tène period.

Introduction

In the report sent to his king from Acre in 1255 the Franciscan friar William of Rubruck, in reference to his travels in the Crimea, says: 'All the way from the Kherson to the mouth of the Tanais there are high mountain peaks along the coast, and there are forty villages between Kherson and Soldaia, of which almost every one has its own language. Dwelling here were many Goths, whose language is German . . .' Three centuries later, in about 1554, Augerois de Busbeck, a French traveller, came across a people he described as Goths on the shores of the Black Sea in the Crimea. After careful analysis of their language from examples surviving at the time of their discovery, philologists identified it as Gothic, with some alteration due to Slavonic influence. This people is now no longer traceable.

These chance references to all that remained of the once numerous and powerful Gothic nation cannot now be verified by the sophisticated anthropological methods available to us today. Thankfully, however, extensive skeletal evidence, not only of the Goths but of many other ancient Germanic peoples from the migration period, does exist. This fact has allowed anthropologists to establish the racial identity of peoples we would otherwise know by name only—colourless wraiths of the imagination.

During the thousand years before the Christian era two great Indo-European peoples, the Celts and Scythians, expanded into central and northern Europe—the Celts to the west, the Scyths to the east. They were followed by two more such groups—the Germans to the west, the Slavs to the east. Both the latter Indo-European groups were to have lasting effects on their chosen areas of settlement, and, later, throughout the planet—especially the Germans.

The period of Germanic migration, the Volkerwanderung, does not begin properly until the 3rd century. However, some see in the eventually abortive invasion of Roman Italy by a marauding Celtic horde the first southward probe involving Germanic warriors. These Cimbri and Teutones had destroyed several Roman armies in a series of encounters throughout Gaul between B.C. 114 and 102. The series of migrations did not end until the adoption of Christianity by the Norwegians in the 11th century A.D.. Germanic homelands comprised modern Denmark, southern and central Norway, the north German coastal strip from the mouth of the Elbe to the Baltic shore, and the islands of Gotland and Bornholm. It was from these breeding grounds that warlike tribes, driven by pressures brought about by overpopulation, began their wanderings. Some have lost their names, being quickly absorbed into bigger Germanic groupings during the ensuing chaos. Populating the dank and gloomy forests of northern Europe, the German 'barbarians' who overran the western Empire were descendants of peasants who had taken up arms; at the time Tacitus wrote his *Germania* in the late 1st century A.D., a large proportion of the male population were warriors, tribal structure was in a state of flux, and their society was moving towards a crisis. Successful war leaders, normally elected only for the duration of a single campaign, were becoming accepted in a permanent capacity as chieftains. The success of many leaders attracted other tribal war bands and, in an era of constant warfare, the transition from tribe to supertribe, grouped under cunning warlords, was well under way.

These vigorous northern 'barbarians' were the destroyers of the Western Empire of Rome. It was they who delivered the *coup de grâce* to the dying colossus in the south, subsequently creating medieval Europe, the feudal system and chivalry. It was their direct descendants who were the knights and men-at-arms. In every sense, they were the creators of the modern world; it is ironic that most of us know virtually nothing about them.

The Warrior

An essential factor in early Germanic and Celtic warfare was the warrior's own large, powerful frame. The German proper was a variant of the earlier Nordic type introduced by the Indo-European invasion; he was, in general, larger, due to racial mixture with the great northern hunters still surviving in northern Europe from the last Ice Age. The body was heavier and thicker than the pure Nordic type, with a large braincase. He was characteristically blond or rufous, as seen in his modern descendants and noted by numerous early writers. The two exceptions to this general picture were the Alemanni and the Franks, who resembled the people they eventually settled among, the Celts.

Diet was heavy and rich in protein, broadly including pork, beef and fish (fresh and salted), mutton, venison, game, bread, beer and dairy produce.

Everyday dress varied from group to group. The overall costume, however, was the same throughout the north—a simple tunic, long trousers and cloak, which was usually of a blackish or dark brown wool. The tunic reached the knees and had either long or short sleeves. Several tunics could be worn at once, supplemented with fur and pelts of different kinds in cold weather. In summer, of course, upper garments were often left off altogether. Linen was known but was an

Longbows found at Nydam and dated to the late 4th century A.D.; about 2m long and made of yew, they bear a close affinity to the great English warbow of the Middle Ages. The arrows, of pinewood and hazel, measure between 68cm and 85 cm; they were found in bundles. (Not to scale)

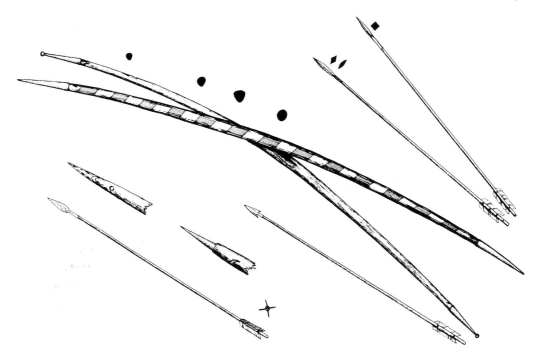

expensive import from the south, and was, for that reason, only worn by the wealthier or far-travelled tribesmen. Trousers were held up by rawhide thonging; sometimes cross-thonging held them into the lower legs or ankles. Trousers were made in wool, as well as fur and skins. Knee-length breeches, when worn, were combined with a tight leg covering. Belts of varied thickness were worn at the waist or across the shoulder, sometimes both. Straps could be used for carrying the shield.

The cloak was about five feet across, rectangular or circular, of woven wool, sometimes having a fur lining. Cloaks entirely of skins were also worn. They were secured with *fibulae* or brooches of differing kinds, some types being more popular among some tribes than others. Clothing of the lower class was of the roughest kind—the simplest woven tunics or dressed skins. Shoes were of a very simple design, in some ways similar to the moccasins of the North American Indian, turned up over the foot from the sole and tied at the ankle.

Hair was often left long, being sometimes plaited, gathered into a top-knot or twisted into the curious knot peculiar to the Suebian tribes such as the Marcomanni and Quadi. Beards were usually but not always worn. Tribesmen normally went bareheaded, but a woollen or fur cap might be worn in cold weather. Razors, combs, scissors and tweezers of early date have been found in Germanic territory. The rough woollen cloth used by the Germans was woven in plain colours, of striped or other geometric design. Dyeing was carried out with vegetable substances, a skill which had existed in the north since the Bronze Age, if not before. Red was obtained from madder root, yellow from saffron flowers and the stalks or leaves of weld, blue from woad, green from what is now known as 'dyers' greenweed'. Many garments were also left in their natural hue—wool has a number of natural shades, ranging from almost pure white, through fawn, brown and grey to black.
Bracelets, earrings, armlets, necklets, beads and rings were worn by both sexes, to a greater or lesser degree, according to taste.

Strong influences from the rich Bronze Age of northern Europe, and also the influence of the Celts and Scythians, were present in Germanic

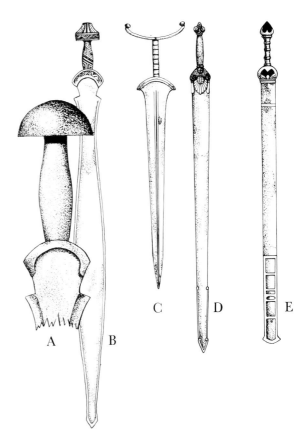

Celtic swords and hilts: (A) 'Mushroom' style pommel, from a large Halstatt sword (B) 'Mexican hat' style pommel from an early Halstatt sword, 108cm long, dated to the 8th century B.C. (C) Late Halstatt iron sword with 'antler' or 'antennae' hilt, 72cm long, 7th century B.C. (D) and (E), La Tène iron swords and scabbards, both 5th to 6th centuries B.C., one 90cm and the other 88cm long.

culture. Roman culture played an ever-increasing part in northern European society after the Celtic collapse in Gaul. In their rôle as a source of weapons and luxury goods, the Romans began their long involvement with the Germans as they faced them across the northern frontiers.

Of the Warrior

'. . . Who these people were and from what part of the world they had set out, to fall on Gaul and Italy like a thundercloud, no one knew; for they had no contact with the southern races, and had already travelled a very great way. The likeliest guess seemed to be that they were some of the German tribes, whose territory extends up to the northern ocean. This conjecture was based on their great size, the light blue colour of their eyes, and the fact that the German word for plunderers

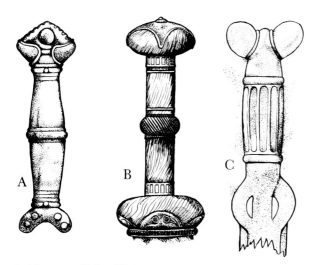

La Tène sword hilts: (A) Solid cast bronze, from Cumberland, England (B) Tinned bronze fittings on wood, from Dorset, England (C) From a bas-relief at Pergamon, Turkey.

is "Cimbri". . . . As for the barbarians, they were so full of confidence in themselves and of contempt for their enemies that they went out of their way to give, quite unnecessarily, exhibitions of their strength and daring. They went naked through snow-storms, climbed to the summits of the mountains, through the ice and snow drifts, and, from there, came tobogganing down on their broad shields, sliding over the slippery slopes and the deep crevasses.' (From the passage on the Cimbri and Teutons, *Fall of the Roman Republic* by Plutarch.)

'. . . The Germans wear no breast plates or helmets. Even their shields are not reinforced with iron or leather, but are merely plaited wickerwork or painted boards. Spears, of a sort, are limited to their front rank. The rest have clubs, burnt at the ends or with short metal points. Physically, they are formidable and good for a short rush. But they cannot stand being hurt . . .' (Part of an eve of battle speech to his troops by Germanicus, 16 A.D.)

'. . . In their war with the Emperor Commodus, the Buri, a small tribe of Germans of the middle Danube, had to ask the Emperor on many occasions for a truce in order to replenish their scanty supply of weapons. They are a tall race, clad in close-fitting garments with a belt round the waist; they hurl their axes and cast their spears with great force, never missing their aim. They manage their shields with great skill, rushing on

their enemy so fast that they seem to fly faster than their javelins.' (Agathius, 405 A.D., writing of the Franks.)

'. . . A Gothic horseman's lance went right through a Roman cavalryman. The Goth slowly raised the dripping lance, with the armoured Roman kicking and vomiting on the end of it.' (Procopius, secretary to the great general of the Eastern Empire, Belisarius, 6th century A.D.)

'. . . Vandal cavalry fight with spear and sword. They have little or no defensive armour, [and] are not good infantrymen, archers or javelineers. Their army was very similar to that of the Ostrogoths, though the Goths had a large infantry force.' (Sidonius Apollinaris. 430–480 A.D.)

'. . . Drinking bouts, lasting a day and night, are not considered in any way disgraceful . . . No one in Germany finds vice amusing, or calls it 'up-to-date' to debauch and be debauched . . . If they approve, they clash spears. No form of approval can carry more honour than praise expressed by arms. . . .'

'. . . On the field of battle it is a disgrace to the chief to be surpassed in valour by his companions or to the companions not to come up in valour to their chief. As for leaving the battle alive after the chief has fallen, *that* means lifelong infamy and shame. To defend and protect him, to put down one's own acts of heroism to his credit, that is what they really mean by allegiance. The chiefs fight for victory, the companions for their chief. Many noble youths, if their land is stagnating in a protracted peace, deliberately seek out other tribes where some war is afoot. The Germans have no taste for peace; renown is easier won among perils, and you cannot maintain a large body of companions except by violence and war. . . .'

'. . . You will find it harder to persuade a German to plough the land and await its annual produce with patience than to challenge a foe and earn the prize of wounds. He thinks it spiritless and slack to gain by sweat what he can buy with blood.' (Tacitus. *Germania*.)

These tantalizing glimpses of north European barbarians, seen through the eyes of civilized southerners, are helpful in giving life to the more immediate relics unearthed by the archaeologist. It should be remembered that not all had witnessed German warriors at first hand; most Romans would have seen their first Germans only if auxiliary troops were posted near their town or had appeared in the arena.

Weapons

Economically the Germanic tribes were peasants, living mainly from stock-rearing (cattle, sheep and goats) and farming. As time went by, isolated farms became groups of farms, developing into hamlets and, eventually, villages. The skills of early German craftsmen showed unaccountable limitations in some directions. This was always evident in the weaponry of the early tribesmen. Roman assessment of the Germanic peoples was, above all, as warriors. With a few notable exceptions, Roman writers had no personal contact with them, and some of their observations may be suspect. Archaeology, however, has supplied a large and detailed amount of German weapon history. Because of the relative paucity of native innovation the Germans, particularly those in the west, were influenced to a large degree by the Celtic Halstatt and La Tène periods of culture. After the Roman conquest of Gaul, Roman weapons played an increasing part in the arming of Germanic war bands, until, in the late Empire, a steady flow of arms northward was sustained by illicit arms deals, loot from Roman arsenals and armies, and equipment brought home by the large numbers of Germans who had served in the Roman army. A broad approximation of phases in weaponry among the ancient Germans, based on recent archaeological evidence, is as follows:

Celtic: Halstatt culture: 7th cent. B.C. Swords of bronze and iron, native iron lances and axes; a period during which very large Celtic weapons were in use—heavy swords, spearheads reaching 75cm in length.

Celtic: Late Halstatt: early 5th cent. B.C. The importance of the sword is overtaken by that of the short, single-edged knife. Ordinary warriors are equipped with a lance and shield of sorts. Javelins furnished with a throwing thong are in use; the axe is more common in eastern German territories.

Celtic: first la Tène culture: late 5th cent. B.C. The

Wooden shields from Hjortspring; the 'barleycorn' bosses are also of wood. These shields, dated to the 1st century B.C., measure 88cm × 50cm, and 66cm × 30cm. Also, two German iron *sax* knives, both about 46cm long.

The northern limits of the La Tène Culture.

15

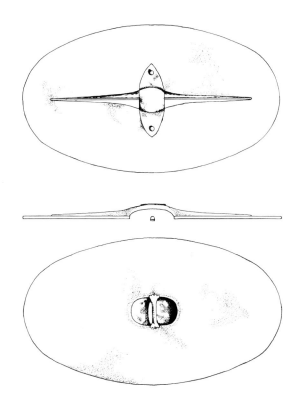

Diagram of an oval Celtic shield made of oak planks, covered with leather and backed with felt; it would probably be finished with a painted design. About 1.1m long, it is 1.2cm thick at the centre and less towards the rim. The spine of shaped wood is hollowed out to receive the warrior's fist as he grasps the handle—normally reinforced with an iron bracing strip—at the rear. The boss itself has an iron reinforcing strip.

(Top to bottom) An Anglo-Saxon *sax*, 6th century A.D.; a Frankish *sax* of the same period; and a rusted iron *sax* about 50cm long, found at Chadlington, Oxfordshire.

beginning of the Celtic La Tène culture sees the Germans in possession of very few swords. The impression gained is that, in parts of Germany, the long sword is virtually unknown. Ordinary warriors are equipped with local variants of spear type, shield and dagger. Spearheads measure 12cm to 26cm.

Celtic: second La Tène phase: 3rd to 2nd cent. B.C. No change in armament evident. At Hjortspring a large wooden boat was discovered preserved in the peat. Classified as a votive deposit and dated to around the late 3rd century B.C., it was accompanied by 138 iron and 31 bone spears, 150 shields and six swords. The shields were all of Celtic patterns—a long, oval type, measuring 88cm × 50cm, and the more common rectangular type, measuring 66cm × 30cm. Towards the end of this period several changes seem to have affected German war bands. The *sax*, a one-edged weapon of varying length, was introduced; its origin is unknown. A few warriors were equipped with La Tène swords—they may have been specialist swordsmen. These men were less common in eastern Germanic territories. The use of Celtic spears, javelins and shields is still evident, the latter with iron bosses. All weapons are light and sparing in the use of iron, confirming an iron-poor society.

Roman period: 1st cent. A.D. Swordsmen number about one in ten among Germanic warriors of this period. There is no evidence of armour or

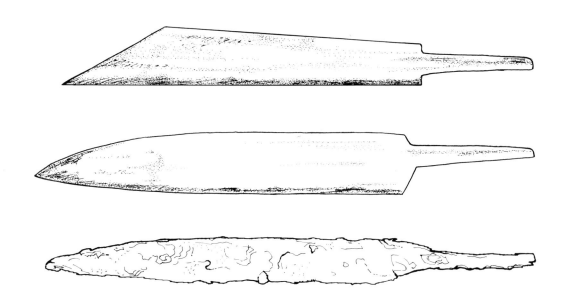

helmets, except in the case of a very few chieftains. Shields are round, rectangular or sexagonal, dished, and with a prominent projecting boss and iron or bronze edging. Small round or oval shields were used by the cavalry.

Roman period: 2nd cent. A.D. Roman and German equipment begins to appear together in a number of areas. Mail garments and Roman swords of the *gladius* type, with ring pommel, and an increase in the use of axes, especially the throwing-axe.

Roman period: 3rd cent. A.D. Roman weapons continue to find their way into northern lands, especially in the more northerly territories. Swordsmen probably number about one in every four warriors. Swords of Roman *spatha* type, together with other Roman types, increasingly find their way into German hands. In the peat bogs at Ejsbol North, 160 shields, 191 spears, 203 barbed javelins, 60 swords, 60 belts and 62 knives were found. Roman cavalry helmets of parade type were used in a few cases probably as marks of rank.

Roman period: 4th cent. A.D. Shields seem to be rarely carried at this period. When found, the bosses are of the Roman domed variety. The old German spiked types are evidently out of fashion.

Owing to widespread cremation of the dead among the northern barbarians the discovered cemeteries, many of them very large, afford little information except for those interested in pottery. Frankish warrior graves in what was northern Gaul and the Rhineland, dated from the mid-4th to the 5th century A.D., are furnished with spears, throwing-axes and an occasional sword. These warriors were probably federate soldiers employed by the Romans. One richly furnished grave of a Germanic officer found in a late Roman cemetery contained a sword, a belt, an oval silver plate and a shield originally covered with purple leather and gold foil plates; the boss had been sheathed in silver-gilt. Other weapons included were a throwing axe, ten spears and a larger spear inlaid with silver. Other Frankish graves in Belgium contain belt fittings and buckles, spears and throwing-axes.

Bows

Well-made longbows were found at Nydam, in the territory of the Angles. They are about two metres long, made of yew, with stave ends tipped with iron or antler ferrules, and the hand-holds bound with fine thread. Arrows were about 68cm to 85cm long.

Germanic bows, dating from about 100 A.D. to 350 A.D., were made of yew and fir wood. They were recognisable long bows of deep 'D' section. It is probable that, like the English longbow of later ages, these were 'compound' bows a combination of the sapwood, which resists stretching, for the back, and heat-wood, resistant to compression, for the belly or inside of the bow. Staves found at Vimose, Kragehul and Nydam measure from 168cm to 198cm. Although used only to a limited degree by Germanic groups in the British Isles, and even less by those settled in Gaul, the bow was used to advantage by other Germans.

As stated above, self bows and a few composite bows were used by the Alemanni. True longbows were present in northern bog deposits. Dated from the 2nd to the 4th centuries A.D., these weapons were probably developed by the Germans themselves. Some arrow piles found seem to be designed to puncture armour.

(Left and right) A Roman cavalry sword of unusual shape, and its scabbard, from Gotland; between them, the hilt of a Roman *gladius* from Thorsbjerg.

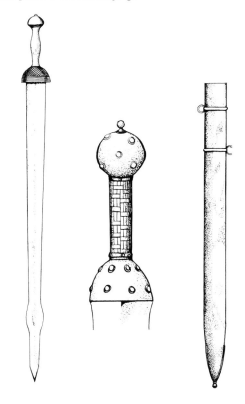

Roman cavalry sword, length 102cm overall; and below it, a Roman *gladius* with the late 'ring' pommel, length 60cm overall. Both are dated to about the 2nd century A.D. and were found at Vimose in Denmark.

A large part of the Visigothic army, as mentioned elsewhere, were archers and spearmen. Their cavalry were composed of chieftains and their companions.

Bowmen also formed an important element in Ostrogothic armies; as with other German bowmen, a very small number of composite bows may have been used, but the overwhelming majority would be self or compound bows. (Their cavalry were armed with spears and swords derived from those of the Sarmatians; Ostrogothic nobles owned lavish, gold-decorated, heavy slashing swords, mounted with almondins.) The longbows found at Vimose, Kragehul and Nydam, dated to 100–350 A.D., have previously been noted. The bow used extensively by all steppe nomads, including the Sarmatians and Huns, was the powerful, reflexed, composite bow. Its stave is constructed of laminated materials of different origin, such as wood, sinew and horn. When unstrung the bow forms the silhouette of the letter 'C', sometimes with the ends forming a cross. When strung, the 'C' was opened back

(Top) A long, heavy Gothic cavalry sword from Tamin in southern Russia, 5th century A.D.—partly restored in this sketch. (Bottom) A sword recovered from Kragehul Bog, Denmark; it has bronze scabbard mounts and hilt, and is dated to the 5th century A.D. (Not to scale.)

against its natural curve and held that way by the string—thus, the bow 'coiled' for action.

Early Swords

Early Celtic iron swords follow the general pattern of previous bronze examples, which were still in use well after the introduction of iron. The first iron swords manufactured in Europe were long, slashing weapons; in the opinion of most experts, they were primarily designed for use by chariot-borne warriors. Some of the weapons belonging to the Halstatt culture were so large that there is some doubt that they were made for actual use. The hilts are generally very distinctive, having a pommel similar to a Mexican hat. Examples include hilts of horn or ivory, decorated with gold or amber, a few have a mushroom-like profile.

Late Halstatt swords, introduced about B.C. 600, were fashioned after examples of Greek or Etruscan provenance; some indeed may be imports from the south. They were smaller than the great middle Halstatt swords, and were designed to be used for both slashing and stabbing, in that they carried a point. Their hilts fall into two main patterns, 'antennae' and 'anthropomorphic'. The former followed an old late Bronze Age pattern; the latter took the stylised form of a spreadeagled man. The blades of these weapons were made of iron, forged to harden by introducing carbon in various ways, finishing with a carburised

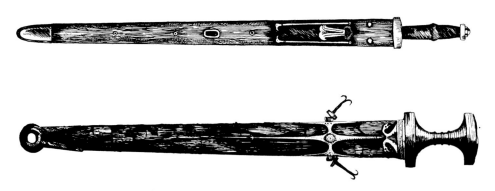

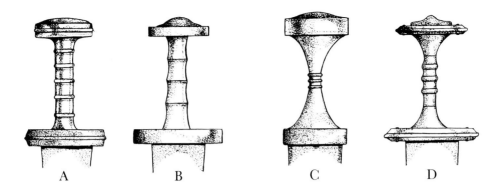

iron of indifferent quality. Although there are notable exceptions, most Celtic swords were made in this way.

Early La Tène swords were introduced about B.C. 450. They have pointed blades about 55cm to 65cm long; there is one known example 80cm long. *La Tène (II) period swords* date from c. B.C. 250 to 120. They measure about 75–80cm and have rounder points. *The final La Tène phase swords*, dated from B.C. 120 to the defeat of the Gallic tribes by Rome, were longer than those of the two previous periods. They are between 60cm and 90cm long; a few were pointed but most were blunt-ended.

Pattern Welded Blades

In the early 1st century A.D. a new process, which we call pattern-welding, was invented by European swordsmiths. The process was complicated, but not so long drawn out as many earlier tempering methods. The central section of the blade was prepared by forging narrow billets of high-quality carburised iron, twisting them together in pairs, laying the twists side by side, welding them, and finally adding further strips of carburised iron to the sides and welding them to form the cutting edges. At this stage the blade was a long, flat, oblong billet, which had to be filed and ground down to the desired form. It was then burnished and etched with an acid such as tannin, urine, sour beer or vinegar; when the central section and fuller were polished, a pattern having the appearance of a snake's back emerged, a result of the twisting carried out at an earlier stage in the sword's manufacture. According to the method used in this grouping and twisting phase, many variations of pattern were possible.

Sword rings and 'life-stones'

On the pommels of some of these swords, rings, mostly decorated, are attached. These are believed to be special gifts from a grateful chieftain. Some scabbards have large beads attached to them, either of pottery, glass, meerschaum, crystal or, rarely, gold set with stones, and occasionally with gold or silver mounts. These are amulets—charms to bring good luck—and were believed to have the magical property to heal wounds made by the sword to which they were attached.

Swords of the Heroic Period

'When the enemy had taken possession of two camps and an immense booty, they destroyed, under new and strange oaths, all that had fallen into their hands. The clothes were torn and thrown away, gold and silver thrown into the river, the ring armour of the men cut to pieces, the accoutrements of the horses destroyed, the horses themselves thrown into the water, and the men, with ropes around their necks, suspended from the trees, so that there was no more booty for the victors than there was mercy for the conquered.'

This extract from a history written about B.C. 100, by the Roman historian Orosius, deals with the Celtic invasion by the Cimbri and Teutones. It highlights the religious obligation felt by the Celts and Germans to sacrifice 'killed' enemy possessions, leaving us with priceless deposits in the bogs of northern Europe to supplement those found in the graves of Germanic warriors. Swords of this period are found in both types of deposit,

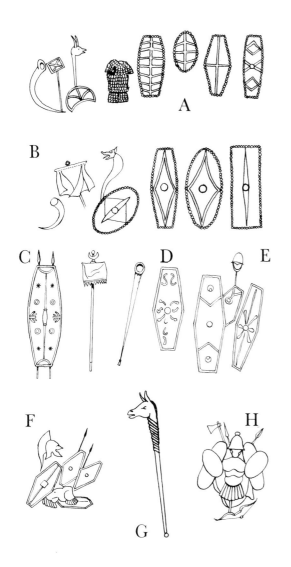

but are present in comparatively few graves.

Roman swords are represented in the bog finds by the short *gladius* and long cavalry *spatha*. One interesting hilt, belonging to a Roman *gladius*, was found at Thorsbjerg, South Jutland. It is similar to one in the British Museum and another found at Pompeii. Its bronze hilt has little bosses on guard and pommel, with a grip covered in fine woven bronze thread braiding. Another example, complete with its scabbard, was found in Gotland. It has a swelling on either side of the blade, just above the point. *Gladii* dated to the 2nd century A.D. have pommels in the shape of a large ring. Several Roman cavalry swords have turned up in the bog deposits.

Besides the Roman swords, Thorsbjerg produced swords of native manufacture. All are double-edged, with bronze- and silver-covered wooden handles. The wooden scabbards bore metal mounts. Also found were a thick sword belt; bronze and iron belt buckles; bows, arrows and shields. These latter were circular and flat, measuring 54cm to 108cm in diameter, with most grips and fastenings of bronze but some of iron. Axes found in this deposit were mounted on wooden shafts 59cm to 85cm long; spears were mounted on shafts 81cm, 250cm, 273cm and 295cm long. Harness for both driving and riding was found, together with much jewellery, tools, amber dice, bowls, spoons, jugs and knives. Garments included mail shirts, gold-plated bronze circular pectoral plates, and a converted Roman cavalry parade helmet covered in silver. Roman coins found included some of Septimus Severus, dated 194 A.D.

At Vimose in Denmark 67 swords were found; most were double-edged, but some were single-edged *saxes*. Of 1,000 spears, five were mounted on shafts 198cm, 264cm, 280cm, and 302cm long; some of these spears had inlays of gold, silver and bronze. Mail was recovered, some of it gilded, together with a complete mail shirt 92cm long; there were also examples of scabbard furniture,

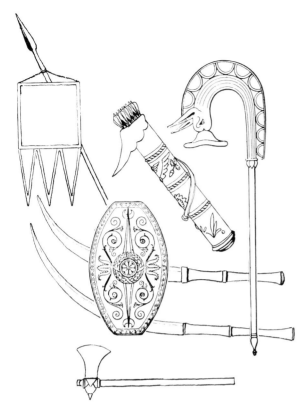

150 knives, buckles, fibulae, buttons, harness, scythe blades, keys, scissors, needles, nails, a millstone, an anvil, hammers, chisels, files, pincers, combs, brooches, beads and four amber dice. This find is dated to the late 4th century A.D.

At Kragehul, also in Denmark, were found ten pattern-welded swords, with spears set in a circular fence. The find is dated to the 4th and 5th centuries A.D.

The four-ship burial at Nydam is of great importance. It contained two small ships which were beyond reconstruction, and two larger ones in a much better state of preservation. Among the associated finds were 106 double-edged swords, 93 of them pattern-welded; silvered sheaths and bone and cast bronze hilts; 552 spears, some inlaid with gold, and arrows. All dated from 200 A.D. to 350 A.D.

Most Germanic swords fall into one or other of the classifications worked out by the Swedish expert Elis Behmer; the hilts of four types occurring frequently in our period are illustrated.

ABOVE **Dacian arms and standards, from various Roman bas-reliefs: not to scale. A dagged banner on a spear; two battle-scythes**—*falxes*; **a quiver, shield and battleaxe; and a carnyx-style standard with a ferrule.**

Helmets from Dacia and Asia.(A)–(E): 'Phrygian' type, from the pedestal of Trajan's Column. (F) and (G): Phrygian helmets. (H) Sarmatian helmet, from Trajan's Column. (I) and (J): Domed helmets, from the pedestal of Trajan's Column. (Not to scale.)

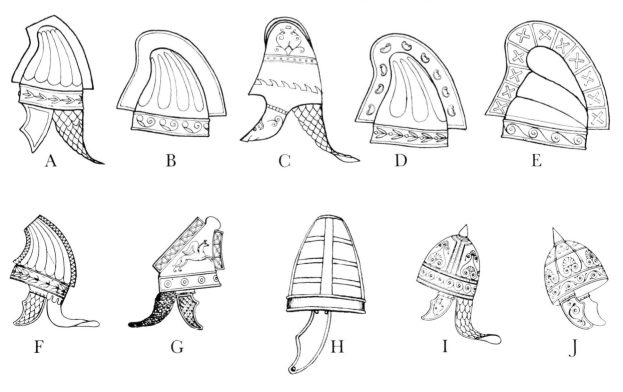

A B C D E

F G H I J

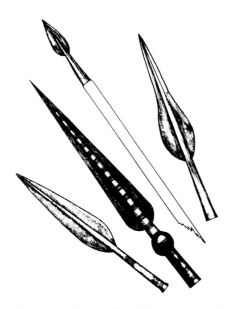

German iron spearheads, 4th to 6th centuries A.D.

Dacian Arms and Armour

The column erected in the Forum of Rome and dedicated to the Emperor Trajan in 113 A.D. illustrates in a spiral ribbon of reliefs the phases and main incidents of his conquest of Dacia. The square pedestal at the base of the column carried examples of arms and armour in confused abundance. The monument, in two halves, can best be seen in England at the Victoria and Albert Museum, where excellent full-scale plaster casts exist. They were taken during the 19th century, and give a

Helmets from the tomb-carvings of A. Julius Pompilius, 175 A.D., at the time of the Marcomannic Wars. (A) Roman battle helmet (B) Damaged carving of Roman cavalry sports helmet (C) Curious helmet of indistinct type. These are thought to depict helmets worn by the enemy in this campaign.

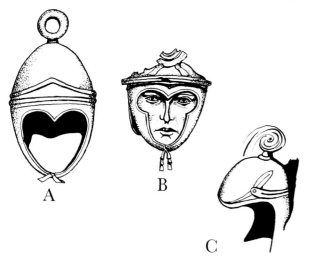

better presentation of the reliefs than the more corroded original in Rome. On confronting the highly-decorated, carved sides of the pedestal, it becomes obvious that the formal abbreviations of costume and weapons used on the column are absent: on the column we have narrative, on the pedestal we are looking at graphic examples of the masses of equipment captured by Roman forces from their opponents in Dacia, sculpted from actual examples of the trophies. In their original condition the bas-reliefs were painted in realistic colours, with details of armour and weapons added in metal. Periodic renewal of the paint was carried out during the life of the Empire.

The cluttered abundance of these impressive trophies begs the question 'Which piece of equipment belongs to which group of barbarians involved in the campaigns?' Perhaps a more relevant question is 'Are the carvings in fact representative of the arms of only one people, the gifted and proud Geto-Dacians, who Trajan had destroyed during a deliberate campaign of Roman expansion into central Europe?' Ancient Dacia, in the 2nd century, embraced Transylvania, Banat and Valachia proper. The true Dacians were a people of Thracian descent. German, Celtic and Iranian elements occupied territories in the north-western and north-eastern parts of Dacia. Cultural elements of Hellenic, Scythian, Celtic and Roman origin were absorbed in a rich amalgam.

Shields

The dominant articles on the pedestal reliefs are the large, richly decorated, oval shields. They are the only type of body shield shown; all are of uniform shape and style of decoration. The exceptions are examples which are covered in a scale pattern. Another example of an unusual Dacian design is found on an oval shield carried by a man in Dacian costume on another Trajanic relief which was moved to the Arch of Constantine. It has four monster-headed trumpets radiating from the central boss, and two Celtic-type torques of twisted metal which, together with the monster trumpets shown in groups all over the pedestal, may illustrate Celtic influence.

With these exceptions, Dacian shields, as shown on the carvings, are heavily decorated with floriate, braided, geometric and planetary designs, as well as the ancient Thracian shield

(Left) A tombstone at Dollendorf near Bonn, shows this Germanic warrior—probably a Frank. He is combing his hair, and his sword is clearly shown; both were considered virility symbols, and were proudly displayed. (Right) Finely sculpted profile of a German chieftain from the tomb of A. Julius Pompilius, now in the National Museum, Terme.

BELOW Late Roman military belt fittings. (Top) This example of ancillary strap attachments and stiffeners is from a grave at Dorchester, England. Probably general issue by the late Empire period, they are usually associated with German auxiliary troops of the Roman army. (Bottom) A reconstructed belt, with strap attachments, stiffeners and plates, from a German warrior's grave at Rhenan, Holland.

known as the *Pelta* (this symbol is used in normal and distorted form). These shields are very large and, it would appear from the carvings, flat, the patterns being in proud relief to facilitate periodic painting. The bosses are hemispherical with round boss plates, both being decorated. I suggest that the Thracian lunate shield motif, repeatedly used on these shields, confirms them as Dacian or Geto-Dacian.

Helmets

The helmets on the reliefs fall into two categories: one with a neat, rounded, cone-shaped shell, the other with its apex curved forward into the characteristic 'Phrygian' peak. Both are highly decorated in the same fashion as the shields on the column base. It is the decoration on one of the solid crests running over one of these helmets, together with the close general resemblance to various examples of helmets worn by ancient Phrygians shown in art, and the obvious connection between them, which leads me to suggest that the 'Phrygian'-type helmets may well be a variety peculiar to the Dacians.

The Dacians, as stated above, were a Thracian

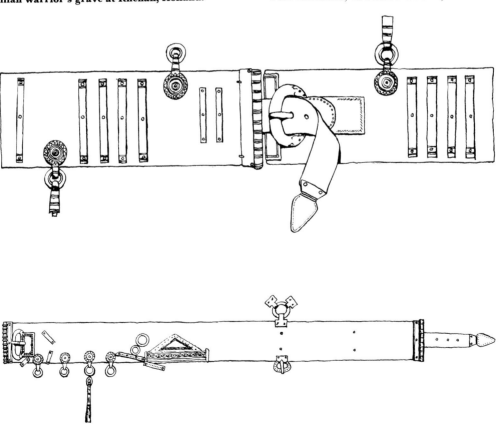

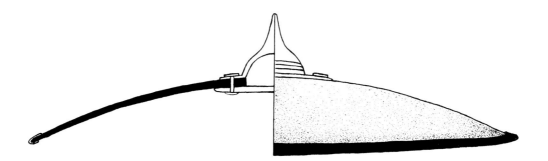

Diagram of an Anglo-Saxon shield, typical of the round shields carried by other Germanic tribesmen. Made of limewood, it is about 5cm thick and 90cm across. Thin, shaped boards were covered with linen or leather; the central recess, with an off-centre metal handle, was covered with a large iron boss; and the rim was of iron or bronze, perhaps sometimes of leather. As well as the concave type, flat, round shields were also used. The face was often reinforced with metal strips, and normally painted with simple or elaborate decorations.

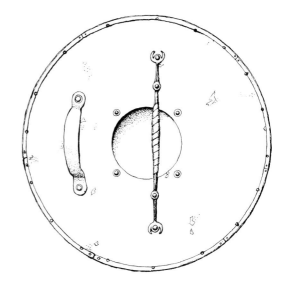

Reconstruction of the inside of an Anglo-Saxon shield, showing forearm strap and hand-grip.

people, as were the Phrygians and those Thracians living north of the Greek states throughout the classical period. The distinct lunate shield used by Thracian infantrymen, the *pelta*, illustrated frequently in Greek art, is present on the solid crest of a 'Phrygian'-type helmet as a running pattern, as shown on the pedestal reliefs; this motif was used repeatedly on the large oval shields. It would be very neat to see in the plainer, domed helmets Scytho-Sarmatian examples, but they resemble the construction of these in only one way—they are conical. The helmets worn by Iranian armoured horsemen on the column and other Roman reliefs are of a composite construction. The banded floriate designs decorating the non-'Phrygian' helmets on the pedestal duplicate the designs shown on the 'Phrygian' helmets. That these helmets represent a newer type of Dacian helmet is a more probable proposition.

Body Armour
This is represented in three varieties—mail, leaf-scale and banded construction. These examples give no indication of their origin or ownership at the time of capture, with the possible exception of the corselet of banded armour, which may not be European.

Dacian Costume
This is more easily identified in the tunic and cloak outfits seen worn on the column and depicted among the trophies on the pedestal. Dacians are not seen on the column wearing body armour or

helmets. Lack of any defence other than the shield must have been characteristic of most of the Geto-Dacians but not of the whole nation, although all are shown unarmoured in a conventional style. Swords are well represented on the reliefs. One weapon, of late Celtic La Tène type, hangs from a belt on a coat of leaf armour. Other long swords with plainer, *spatha*-type guards and hilts have plated belts attached to the scabbard.

The *draco*, a metallic standard in the form of a dragon head with its mouth open, attached to a tubular, fabric body of brilliant hue, was used by many ancient peoples including Dacians, Iranians and Germans. Those shown on the pedestal could belong to any of these groups. *Vexilla*, ancient banners, shown on the column friezes and pedestal, may be examples of recaptured Roman *signa*, or may belong to any of the participating barbarians. One example, attached to a spear,

Reconstructed drawings of two Saxon warriors: (left) from Lower Saxony, probably an ex-Roman soldier, based on a 4th century grave at Liebenau; (right) a free Saxon warrior of the 5th century, based on grave no. 60 at Petersfinger, Salisbury, England.

looks very un-Roman; it carries three large 'dags' at its lower edge.

Weapons

Spears and javelins are of standard types and give no hint as to their provenance. Battleaxes of a distinct type are present, as are the terrible *falxes*. It is postulated that these scythe-like weapons were so effective in early actions between Roman and Dacian infantry that special Roman armour, based on antique patterns, was devised, and shields were reinforced. Both composite and self bows are present on the reliefs, the self bow being more numerous on the carvings but little-shown on the column, where Dacians and Sarmatians are both shown using reflex bows. Quivers are of a lidded, tubular shape, highly decorated. Trumpets, after the fashion of the Celtic *carnyx*, in the shape of monster serpents, are shown in groups. Some examples, however, seem to be designed as standards for carrying, having a large finial at the butt end.

If this analysis is generally correct, then it would seem that the base of Trajan's Column carries bas-reliefs of armour, arms and other equipment wholly or overwhelmingly belonging to the Dacian people, the target of Trajan's campaigns. Some authorities may see in the presence of various pieces associated with cultures further to the east, especially the coat of banded armour, trophies of erstwhile ownership by Iranian Roxolani. I would agree that this is a reasonable theory; but would it not be possible for leading warriors among the Geto-Dacians to own pieces of armour not made in Europe?

Warfare

Prior to the conquest and pacification of Gaul by Roman forces, German tribes proper began moving south-west. By the early 1st century A.D. they were in the Rhineland area. The people settled at this time between the Aller in the east and the Oise in the west are believed to have been an aboriginal group of 'old' Europeans, neither

The general distribution of major Germanic groups in about 100 A.D.

Wars, Tacitus wrote his *Germania*[1], a study of the Germans written in about 98 A.D. In the passage describing the arming of warriors, he says: 'Only a few have swords or spears. The lances that they carry—*frameae* is the native word—have short and sharp heads, but are so narrow and easy to handle that the same weapon serves for fighting hand to hand or at a distance. The horseman demands no more than his shield and spear, but the infantryman has also javelins for throwing, several to each man, and he can hurl them to a great distance.'

This description accords well with archaeological evidence dated to this time. Whether *frameae* had short, narrow heads by choice or simply because of the tribes' shortage of iron is not made clear by the historian. Bodies found preserved in the peat bogs of northern Europe, dated to this period, are dressed exactly the same as the Germans shown on Roman monumental remains. With the exception of a very few individuals, German body defences—apart from the shield— were non-existent at the time of their early encounters with Imperial troops. The usual tactic adopted at this time was to attack at a headlong rush, in wedge formation, so as to close in quickly, thus nullifying the murderous volleys of legionary *pila*: the 'Furore Teutonicus' of legend.

Celtic nor Germanic, speaking a pre-Indo-European tongue. Their replacement by a more pugnacious people was almost certainly recognized by Roman frontier intelligence, which may have triggered the Augustan campaigns. Tribes such as the Chatti, Cherusci, Chamavi, Chattvarii, Chamari, Angrivarii, Ampsivarii, etc., were followed by the Alemanni, Goths, Gepids, Franks, Vandals, Bajuvara, Thuringians and Saxons.

Probably drawing heavily on the experiences of men returned from the German campaigns of Augustus, and on Pliny the Elder's *The German*

In the early years of the 1st century A.D. Rome decided to rationalise the northern frontier by annexing Germany up to the Elbe. The closing move, against the Marcomanni, was frustrated when the new provinces in north Germany flared into revolt. The three legions stationed in the area, the XVII, XVIII and XIX, were annihilated in a series of ambushes in the Teutoburger Wald in 9 A.D. The German leader, Hermann (Arminius), chief of the Cherusci, had served in the Roman army and had used his knowledge of its operational limitations in boggy, heavily wooded areas. Hermann aspired to more permanent power than that afforded to a war leader, and was subsequently destroyed by political enemies at home. The indisputable outcome of this disaster was that Roman plans for the eventual control of all of Germania were permanently abandoned.

Two iron axeheads, the elevations on the left from a find at Brandenburg, and those on the right from a find at Weissenfels.

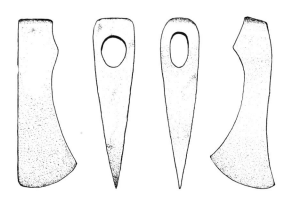

[1] Pliny's book is now lost; this is the more tragic since we know that the author had himself served on the frontier.

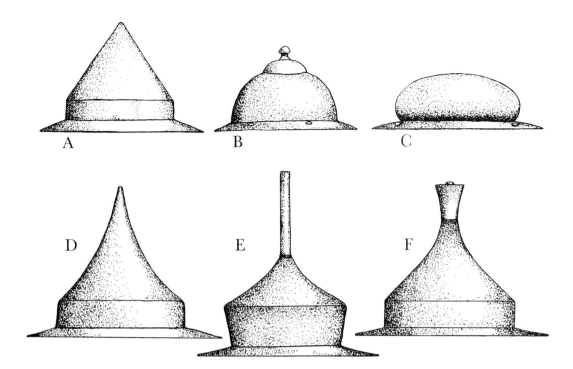

German iron shield bosses from (A) Hamburg (B) Gotland (C) Gotland (D) Hamfelde (E) Vimose (F) Gotland

Germanicus, the nephew of the Emperor Tiberius, conducted a series of short campaigns in Lower Germany, making some amends for the destruction of the three-legion garrison of the area by paying honour to them in their place of death. The Empire was kept within its frontiers and stood on the defensive in the north. Caligula's idiot dreams of conquest in Germany came and went until other antics took his interest.

During the civil wars of 68 to 69 A.D., Gallic tribes of the north-east, with German allies, destroyed Roman forces on the Rhine and announced an 'Empire of the Gauls'. Roman forces moved swiftly to eradicate this Gallic empire. Vespasian and his sons then closed the

'Spangenhelm' composite helmets of the Migration period. (Left) Iron helmet of a Roman auxiliary soldier of the 3rd century A.D., found in Holland. (Centre) Gothic helmet from the battlefield of Tolbiacum, 5th century A.D.; the shell is of iron, with decorative gilded copper skinning. (Right) Helmet from a 6th century warrior's grave in Alsace—probably an heirloom of earlier date.

dangerous gap between the Rhine and Danube with a deep defence system. After Domitian had halted the migrating Chatti on the middle Rhine, during a series of bitterly fought campaigns in 83 and 88 A.D., Upper and Lower Germany settled down to a period of quiet, ably administered by Trajan. Legions could now be transferred from the Rhine to the Danube. Eastern German tribes began to attract Roman military interest when the great Marcomannic chieftain, Maraboduus, created a large confederacy of tribes, after his own people, together with the Quadi, had driven the Boii from Bohemia. He eventually escaped to sanctuary in Ravenna in 17 A.D., when fellow Germans reacted against his growing power.

Thracians

During the great migrations of an earlier period, Indo-European groups of warriors and their families moved into large areas of Europe. One of these closely related groups occupied territory in south-eastern Europe and, eventually, parts of the Near East and east-central Europe. These were the Thracians. In the 1st century the Thracians of southern Europe were separated from their more northerly kin, the Dacians. The Thracians within the Roman frontier became famous for their recruitment into the Roman cavalry.

German standards: (Left) from the tomb of A. Julius Pompilius, the Aurelian general—possibly also a trumpet? (Right) a vexillum-type standard, from an Augustan coin reverse.

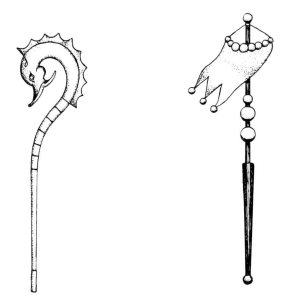

Sarmatians

In the vast Russian steppe, a group of mounted Indo-Europeans, known as Iranians, lived a highly developed nomadic life. They had moved into areas vacated by those Indo-Europeans now living in Europe. Some had invaded India in about B.C. 1200, others had founded the empires of the Medes and Persians. By about the 5th century B.C., those still living on the Eurasian steppe were the Scythians to the west, with Sarmatians to the east of them and Sakas further to the east. Probably as a result of Chinese operations against nomads on their western frontiers, the steppe was set in motion. The Sarmatians moved west and obliterated the Scythians, whose remnants fled to the Danube and Crimea. By the middle of the 2nd century B.C. the Sarmatians became known in Europe as the Iazyges and Roxolani, and those remaining to the east, the Alans. It is believed that Sarmatian success against the Scythians was due to the creation of a force of super-heavy cavalry, both man and horse being completely armoured in some of the formations. These 'cataphracts' operated as a shock force alongside the traditional horse-archer formations used by all mounted nomads.

Neither Thracians nor Sarmatians were Germans. The reasons for their mention in this small work are several. The Dacians were a Thracian people, but Dacia was occupied also by Daco-Germans, and in the north-east by Celto-Dacians. The Sarmatian Roxolani became firm allies of the Dacians, supplying them with the only heavy cavalry force in the Dacian army. With the destruction of Dacia, Rome brought her forces into direct contact with the eastern German tribes, an area which was, in due time, overrun by the German Gepids. In 85 A.D., Dacian forces attacked Roman defences in Moesia, harrying the countryside and killing the Governor. The Emperor Domitian commanded initial operations to clear Moesia of invaders, but later passed control of the operations to Cornelius Fuscus. The campaign was carried into eastern Dacia, but the weight of Dacian numbers gradually drove the Roman forces back, and, in a final battle, they were wiped out, Fuscus suffering the fate of his army. Roman military honour was restored to some degree by the battle of Tapae, in 89 A.D.,

German warriors, 1st century BC-1st century AD

A

Dacian warriors, 2nd century AD

B

Marcomanni and Quadi, 1st-2nd centuries AD

Gothic warriors, 4th century AD

D

Gothic warriors, 4th century AD

E

Frankish warriors, 5th century AD

'Anglo-Saxon' warriors, 5th century AD

2 1 3

German soldiers of Roman Army, 4th-5th centuries AD

H

where the Dacians were thoroughly beaten. Decabalus, the King of Dacia, was forced to pay an annual tribute to Rome and to allow Roman armies passage through Dacian territory. That the Emperor did not recognise the victory as conclusive is borne out by the fact that he refused the title of 'Dacicus' at this juncture.

In 98 A.D., the Emperor Trajan came to power. The situation he inherited was one of increasing unease about the northern frontiers. Rome faced constant threat from German tribes in the west; and the Dacians were expanding their strongholds, it was believed, in readiness for another attack. Dacian culture at this time was far in advance of that of their fellow European barbarians. It was, in all recognisable aspects, an embryo civilization. Towns were beginning to develop from the great defended strongholds called *oppida*, such as the capital at Sarmizegethusa. Centres of importance were defended by minor *oppida* and other outposts. Trade was well organized and encouraged; silver and gold work, pottery, iron implements and weapons, of extremely high quality, were produced for home consumption and export to the sophisticated Roman world in the south. It was this nascent civilization which now attracted increased Roman military interest.

In the winter of 100–101 A.D., Trajan massed ten legions, vexillations of other legions, and huge numbers of auxiliary troops of all kinds at Viminacium, a military base on the south bank of the Danube. The Roman army of conquest crossed the Danube on pontoon bridges, into Dacian territory, in the spring of 101 A.D. No opposition was offered until the army reached the general area of Tapae, where they were confronted by a large Dacian force. The ensuing battle was indecisive. The Dacians retreated to the mountains, killing livestock and burning crops to delay the Roman advance. After a further advance the Roman forces settled into winter quarters. The Dacians, together with their Sarmatian allies, the Roxolani, mounted an attack in Lower Moesia which was repulsed by the Romans. During the winter the Romans occupied themselves with carrying out marvels of engineering.

In the spring of 102 A.D., the Romans attacked Sarmizegethusa through the Red Tower Pass.

During the whole of this period Dacian emissaries were sent to Trajan, who constantly refused them audience. Finally receiving a deputation of prominent nobles, he sent them back with terms which the Dacian king, Decabalus, refused. After a further major battle Decabalus surrendered and Roman forces occupied the Dacian capital, Sarmizegethusa.

By 105 the Dacians had re-armed, taking the Roman garrison commander of Sarmizegethusa hostage; he in turn, took the initiative away from the Dacians by swallowing poison. Once again the Dacians ravaged the Roman province of Moesia. With great effort the Romans relieved the province before winter closed in. In the spring of 106 the Romans mounted a two-pronged assault on Sarmizegethusa, which they put to siege. When all seemed lost, some nobles took poison; others— including Decabalus—escaped. Those who fled were pursued ruthlessly; Decabalus was sur-

Angons—**heavy Germanic javelins with iron heads and shanks; length, including wooden shaft, was probably about 210cm (7ft). Examples from (left to right) France, Germany, Austria and England. The design was, obviously, intended to kill or cripple efficiently; the length of the iron shank suggests that the** *angon* **was used in hand-to-hand combat, where there was a danger of the head being lopped off. The similarity to the classic Roman** *pilum* **raises the question of whether the** *angon* **was also intended to weigh down the enemy's shield when thrown.**

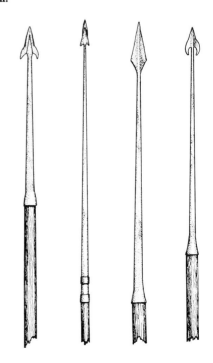

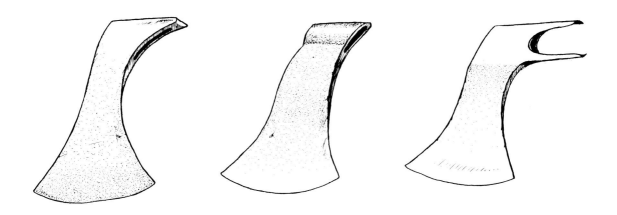

Examples of the *francisca*, **the German throwing-axe, found in northern France and dated to the 4th to 6th centuries A.D.**

rounded, but, before capture, took his own life by cutting his throat. After the reduction of remaining pockets of resistance, large parts of Dacian territory were annexed as a Roman province.

The Marcomannic Wars

By the middle of the 2nd century, pressure on Rome's northern frontier was mounting as the numerical increase among German tribes impelled their leaders to look for new ground. Goths and other German tribesmen began to move south-east in a steady stream. This movement blossomed into the Gothic nation of southern Russia and the Gepid nation of the Carpathians; the Astingi (Asding) Vandals moved into territory west of the Roman province of Dacia, formerly dominated by the Sarmatian Iazyges. The Roman military command must have followed these developments with foreboding. To the north-west, the Rhine tribes were entering into the super-tribe status of permanent federation. As early as the 1st century A.D. pressure was building on the middle Danube frontier; Roman strongholds had existed with Dacian agreement in the area since the first conquest of Dacia in 106 A.D., on the left banks of the rivers Danube, March and Thaya. During the winter of 166–7, the Lombards, a west German group, crossed the frozen Rhine, carrying with them the Lacringi, Victofali and Ubii. They were immediately followed by a breakthrough of Marcomanni, Quadi and Sarmatian Iazyges in the central Danube area. From then on a kind of 'blitzkrieg', launched by a barbarian conspiracy, sucked in ever-increasing numbers of barbarians,

in spite of a Roman offensive in 170, directed against the Quadi in particular. Roman armies were by-passed on the left and right flanks, and Greece was invaded. Early in 171 Italy too was subjected to brief invasion, which was quickly nullified by Roman forces rushed from the frontier areas. Later in the year Marcus Aurelius rid the Empire of invaders, and peace was negotiated with the Quadi and Iazyges. In 172 the Marcomanni were attacked by Roman forces on the Danube. The Quadi, breaking their treaty with Rome, assisted their Suebian kinsmen. After defeating the Marcomanni, Marcus turned to the Quadi, who were attacked and defeated in 173. The Quadi then made peace. In 174, Roman troops attacked the Iazyges, whereupon the Quadi broke their treaty once more. The war continued into 175, until an armistice was declared in the summer of that year.

During these vicious wars, serious weaknesses in the defences of the north were exposed. The Empire had been invaded and devastated. The constant fighting had made extremely heavy demands on the army at all levels, and, at one point, the gladiatorial schools were emptied in a desperate experiment. The struggle with Rome during the Marcomannic wars had brought far-reaching changes to the Germanic peoples, and created in them an eagerness to launch more assaults on the colossus in the south. Sixteen of Rome's 33 legions manned the northern frontier, together with large numbers of auxiliary troops, at the end of the Marcomannic wars—an end which proved to be only a beginning for the Germans.

The tribes most closely involved in these wars,

the Marcomanni and Quadi, were Germans belonging to the Suebian group of tribes. These Germans had become relatively civilized after a long period of contact with Noricum and Pannonia. Their close knowledge of the operational system and eager acquisition of the technology of the Roman army made these tribes formidable opponents.

The Goths

From their geographical position the Goths, the most powerful Germanic group, seem to have been the last of that family to settle in Europe. They occupied territory in Scandinavia and what is now northern Prussia, under various names given them by classical writers, such as Gothones and Guttones, Gothini and Getae (Gaudae). Their own name for themselves appears to have been the Gutthinda. To return momentarily to the Dacian wars: a strong component of the Dacian army (including the Celtic Bastarnae and the Germans), rather than submit to Trajan, had withdrawn. They had dispersed or been absorbed, probably by other tribes or even by the Goths during their movements south at a later date. From the latter years of the second century A.D., the Goths were in possession of large tracts of country north of the Danube, on the coast of the Euxine as far east as the Tauric Chersonese or Crimea, deep in territory once belonging to the Sarmatian Roxolani, from whom they learned the use of heavy cavalry, the *kontos* (a large, heavy lance), and the stirrup.

These shock troops, heavy cataphract cavalry, were not completely new. Cataphracts had been in existence among Iranian nomads for centuries. The Sarmatians had perfected their use, which had enabled them to defeat the Royal Scythians and move into control of their territory. The Goths seem to have overthrown the Sarmatians by their ferocity in battle, probably hamstringing the horses (a German tactic). Thus, equipped with a heavy cavalry force to support the masses of traditional infantry, they faced the Roman army of the 3rd century, which was now composed largely of Germans, Illyrians and North Africans.

In the mid-3rd century Goths broke into the Balkans, killing the Emperor Decius (Hostilianus). This was followed, in 256, by a cave-in of the Rhine frontier. Gaul was overrun by the Franks and

Reconstruction of a guardsman of the *Germani Corporis Custodes*, in palace duty dress. These were picked men who formed a personal bodyguard for the emperors from the time of Augustus until about 70 A.D., and again from the early 3rd century onwards. They were often used to counter the ambitions of the Praetorian Guard.

Alemanni, some of them reaching Spain and Italy. The Goths, after exhausting the Balkans, also spread into Anatolia. Their stay in the Balkans was marked by constant defeats by Roman forces led by the Illyrian Emperors.

In 275 A.D. Rome formally abandoned Dacia, which was promptly occupied by the Gepids and

Two iron *franciscas* **recovered in England. (British Museum)**

Mainly at the expense of Slavonic tribes, the great Gothic leader Ermanarich directed a rapid expansion of his Ostrogoths—the eastern Goths—into the Baltic and across the Don, occupying the little Roman protectorate of the Bosporan kingdom. The assassination of Ermanarich brought distracting confusion to the Ostrogoths at a perilous time. In 370 A.D. rumours were reaching them from their eastern outposts that a people of unusually ugly appearance were moving west across the steppe. Ostrogothic expansion in the east had brought them into contact with true nomadic peoples, Iranians and Finns. In the east they had adopted the nomadic way of life. It was possibly this eastern expansion under Ermanarich which had triggered the avalanche of Huns and Sarmatian Alans, which now headed their way.

The Huns, a Turco-Mongol people, had developed a large, powerful, composite bow, an improved version of the traditional weapon used by the nomadic horse-archer. With this they had been able to penetrate the armour worn by Chinese soldiers, thus nullifying the worst effects of the forward policy of Chinese military authorities, which had set them in motion towards the West. The use of this bow had also been instrumental in their defeat of Iranian nomads, the most westerly of whom were the Alans. Here again, Hunnish arrows were able to penetrate armour worn by Iranian cataphracts. The Huns, however, saw the value of using these large numbers of heavy cavalrymen to subsidise their own small force of armoured horsemen. The Goths who now stood in their path had an army consisting of vast numbers of lightly armed bowmen and cavalry, some of whom would be armed in Sarmatian fashion. The Ostrogothic armies were sent reeling in a south-westerly direction, their empire destroyed. The Visigoths fared no better. The Gepids became Hunnish vassals on the Hungarian steppe. Visigoths, Ostrogoths and Astingi Vandals asked for sanctuary within the Roman Empire, and were allotted territory along the Danube by the Emperor Valens. This immense and voracious host crossed into Roman territory and passed straight into the toils of corrupt prefects and merchants, who

the western branch of the numerous Goths, known as the Visigoths. On the Rhine, the angle formed by the Danube in the Black Forest region was also vacated by Rome and occupied by the Alemanni.

Roman troops of the 4th century were finding it no easy matter to defeat a German tribe. Imperial troops lacked the confidence and homogeneity of earlier centuries. Consequently they needed more careful handling in the field. The Germans, by contrast, were organising themselves into super-tribes. New confederacies were now established: the Saxons in the north, Burgundians south of them, Franks north of the Main and the Alemanni to their south. Large formations of the Roman army were made up of Franks, Alemanni, Goths, Vandals, Heruli, Quadi, Marcomanni and Sarmatian Alans. Germans now officered many units, some individuals rising to the highest ranks in the Imperial army. Deserted areas around the frontiers were resettled with ex-prisoners of war from German tribes. More importantly from a military point of view, German tribes were allowed to settle by treaty, under their own chieftains, as 'federates', in return for military service. By way of extension of this policy, clever diplomacy was conducted beyond the frontiers.

Fourteen spearheads, a sword, three iron bosses and an iron *francisca* **head recovered at Croydon, Surrey. (British Museum)**

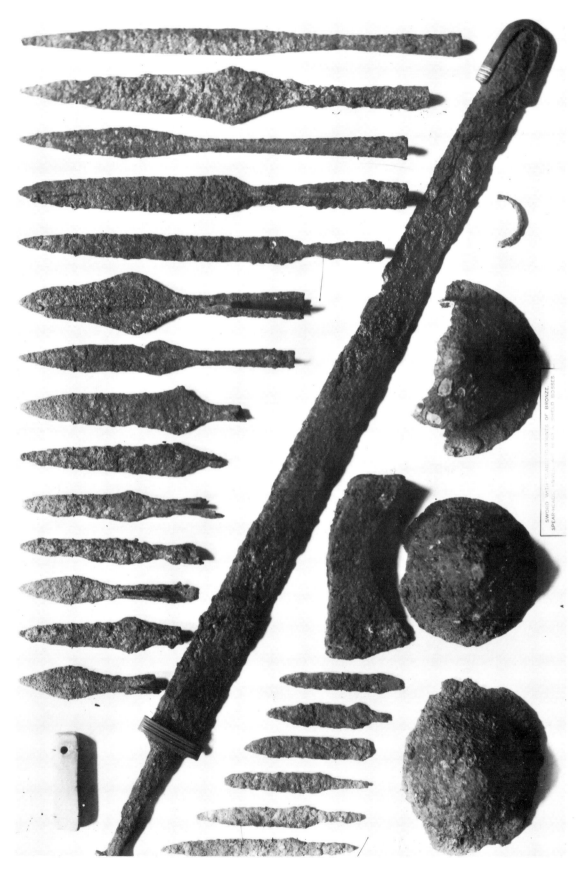

SWORD WITH SCABBARD BRONZE, SPEAR-HEADS, KNIVES, AND SHIELD BOSSES

disarmed them, and charged exorbitant prices for bad grain and rotting meat. As money ran out, slaves were taken in payment for the dog-meat now offered. Gothic patience ran out and, after breaking into Roman arsenals to regain their weapons, they made alliance with the remaining free Alans and invaded Thrace. They were met at Adrianople by the Emperor Valens and the army of the Eastern Empire.

Visigothic and Ostrogothic infantry were in laager behind their wagons and the Ostrogothic cavalry were in the country foraging when the Romans deployed and began the attack on the laager. At this point, the Ostrogothic cavalry appeared back from foraging and charged the right wing of the Romans, whereupon the Gothic infantry left the laager and attacked and broke the Roman cavalry. The Roman infantry were then systematically destroyed. When night fell the remnants were able to escape. The catastrophe at Adrianople in 378 A.D. was the worst defeat for the Roman army since Republican times. Among the dead were the Emperor of the Eastern Empire, Valens, the Grand Master of Cavalry, the Grand Master of Infantry, the Count of the Palace, 35 commanders of different corps, and nearly the whole of the Roman army of the east—estimated at 40,000 deaths.

Six years after Adrianople, Goths, Vandals and other Germans, numbering about the same as those lost in the disaster, were enlisted under their own chieftains as cavalrymen in the army of the East.

Meanwhile the Visigoths, frustrated by their inability to take walled towns, were encouraged to quieten down in 382. They became unsettled again in 396, and were persuaded to resettle in north-west Greece. In 402–3 they invaded Italy, only to be promptly defeated by the army of the

The Roman Empire on the eve of the great Germanic Migrations, in about 395 A.D.

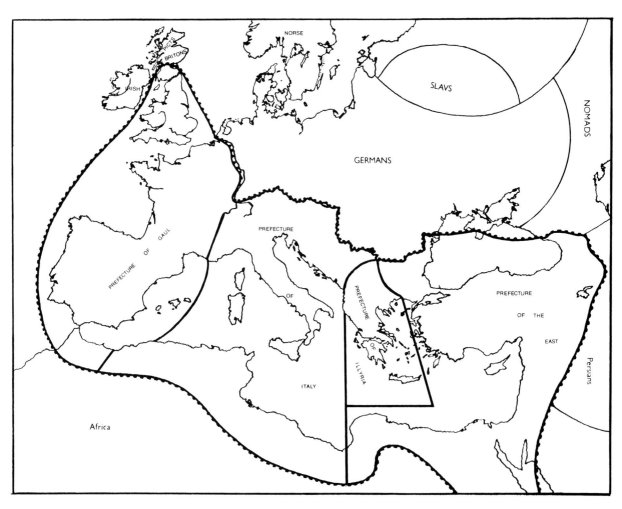

West, commanded by the Romano-Vandal general, Stilicho. In 405 Stilicho defeated a mixed army of Ostrogoths. Quadi and Astingi Vandals with an army which had to be reinforced from units manning the frontier on the Rhine, from Bavaria and Britain. On the last day of 406 another coalition—of Marcomanni, Quadi, Astingi and Siling Vandals—crossed the frozen Rhine into Gaul, accompanied by a clan of dispossessed Sarmatian Alans. Gaul was defenceless and they harried far and wide. After three years they were allowed to cross the Pyrenees into Spain, where they settled on the Atlantic seaboard.

Angles, Saxons and Jutes

German warriors were used extensively in defence of the Empire, and Britain was no exception. Batavian, Frisian, Frankish and Saxon soldiers were used in Britain from the 2nd century, a tradition which the Romano-British continued. In the 3rd and 4th centuries a chain of forts were built around the coastal areas, harried by Saxon raiders, these forts being manned by a special force under the command of the 'Count of the Saxon Shore'. Archaeological evidence from areas previously well populated in north Germany, Denmark and the North Sea coast shows that soon after 400 A.D. an extensive migration had taken place, and continental settlement sites were abandoned. No evidence of villages built after the 4th century exists in some coastal areas. Cremation sites used for 300 years show very limited use; they contain only a few late 5th-century urns. In Danish bogs, votive deposits stop abruptly. In 410 the Saxons attacked Britain in earnest.

At some stage in Saxon involvement with Britain the decision was taken—together with Angles, Frisians, Jutes, and a small number of Franks and Slavonic Wends—to migrate into the rich farmlands of southern Britain. Mercenaries and pirates, fishermen and farmers brought their families over for permanent settlement. Roman troops had been withdrawn to reinforce the Rhine armies fighting desperately to hold the collapsing northern frontier; and the Romanized British were advised, in a letter from the Emperor Honorius, to organize themselves in a programme of self-help, offering freedom to slaves who responded to the call. The Romano-British did indeed organise, in an admirable way, in sharp contrast to the response in Gaul, which was subjugated within 50 years by the Franks. The numbers of barbarians involved may have been greater than those of the Anglo-Saxons, but British resistance was more stubborn. Some Romano-Britons escaped from the south-west,

The hilt of an Anglo-Saxon ring-sword of about the 6th century A.D., found at King's Field, Faversham, Kent. (British Museum)

settling on the Brest Peninsula, where they became known as Bretons. Resistance to the Saxons was so determined in the 6th century that many German migrants returned to their homelands or settled in north-western Gaul, by courtesy of the Franks[1]. In the mid-6th century the Anglo-Saxon advance began again, into Wiltshire and towards the rich prizes of Devon and Somerset, the best farmland in Britain. This was the final phase of the permanent Germanising of a large part of the British mainland. As in other parts of Roman Europe previously, the cities were gradually depopulated until only squatters occupied small precincts. To the German warrior-farmers, cities meant nothing except as places of wonder, built by giants.

Stilicho, the Romano-Vandal, had excited the distrust of the Emperor Honorius because of his vaulting ambition, and was consequently murdered. Once removed, Stilicho could not bargain with the German leaders. Alaric, king of the Visigoths, presented his demands for land subsidies and military command at the gates of Rome. The Roman authorities, now safely resident in Ravenna, refused his requests: this led to an immediate but half-hearted sack of the city. The political effect, however, was devastating. Roman prestige plummeted. The Visigoths marched away to the south with some idea of crossing to North Africa, where they could control Roman corn-lands. In southern Italy, Alaric died, thus enabling undivided Roman attention to be directed northward over the Alps. The Visigoths were finally led out of Italy by Alaric's brother Athaulf, to the Rhineland, where they assisted Roman forces in the pacification of that area. In 414 they trekked into Spain, where, by 416, they had exterminated the Siling Vandals and Alans. The Astingi Vandals and Suebian Germans were saved by Roman intervention. The Visigoths accepted extensive lands in southern Gaul, north of the Pyrenees.

The Empire of Attila

By the 5th century the Huns controlled a vast area of German territory and pasture, once belonging to Iranian nomads, stretching back to the Caspian. In 436 they attacked the Burgundians, who moved into Roman land around Geneva as *foederates* (settled allies).

In 451 Attila led an army composed of Huns, Alans, Goths and other Germans into Gaul. In an inconclusive battle at Campus Mauriacus a mixed army of Romans, Burgundians, Salian Franks and Visigoths checked him. The following year the Huns raided Italy, but were bought off. Attila died in Hungary in 453. After his death the Hunnish Empire split into disunited groups led by the dead Khan's sons. Their German subjects destroyed the Huns in a battle fought at Nedao in Dacia; the remnants were absorbed by the Roman army and by other nomads on the steppe.

While the Romans and other German tribes were occupied with the Huns, the Astingi Vandals invaded North Africa from Spain in 428, where they took over the best provinces and, under King Gaiseric, built a Vandal fleet which turned to piracy. In about 470 the Visigoths descended into Spain, becoming its ruling caste, while still holding territories in Gaul.

De-Germanising the Eastern Army

The Emperor of the East, Zeno (457–474), used Isaurians (semi-civilised Anatolian mountaineers) in the Imperial Guard, and formed new regiments of Isaurians and Armenians. He also induced the Goths remaining in the eastern Empire to migrate to Italy, enabling him to leave his successor an army purged of truculent Germans.

One of the final moves which must be mentioned before closing this survey is that of the Franks, who moved into northern Gaul in 486, expanding into Alemannic and Visigothic territory led by their king, Clovis, who died in 511 A.D.

While the Goths climbed to the zenith of power under their king Theodoric the Great (451–526), the German tribes involved in the great migrations settled down among their Romanised subjects. The last move was made in the 6th century by the Lombards, who, to avoid nomadic pressure, moved west. In 568 they settled in the Po Valley and some lands to the south. The next out-pouring of Germanic peoples began in the 8th century, when they were known as Vikings, Rus, Varangians and Normans.

---

[1] According to the tantalisingly fragmentary accounts, this rolling back of the Germanic invasion was the work of the legendary Arthur.

The Germanic conquest of the Western Roman Empire: Europe in about 476 A.D.

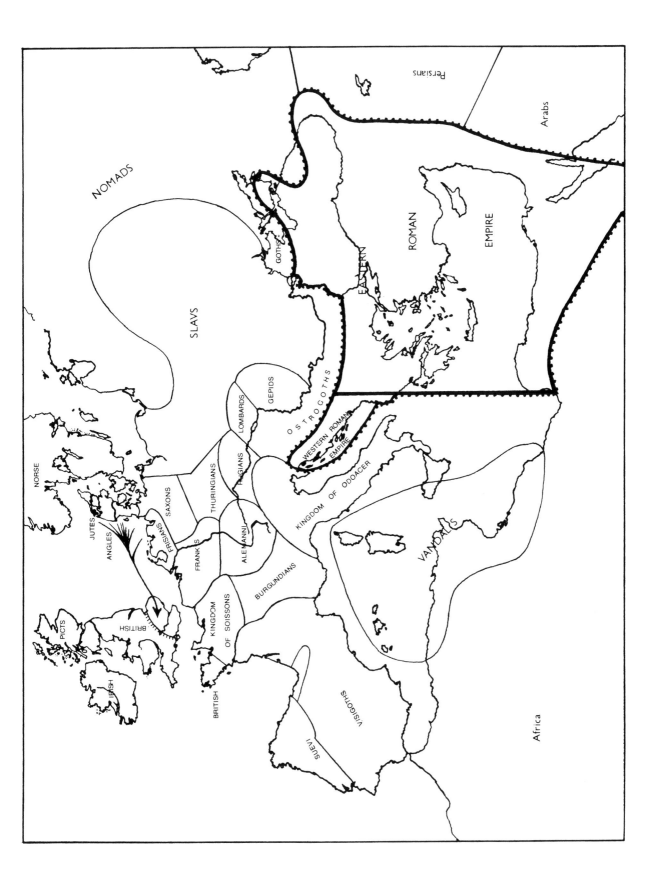

NOMADS

SLAVS

NORSE

PICTS

IRISH

BRITISH

JUTES

ANGLES

FRISIANS

SAXONS

THURINGIANS

FRISIANS

LOMBARDS

GEPIDS

GOTHS

OSTROGOTHS

EASTERN

ROMAN

EMPIRE

Persians

Arabs

FRANKS

ALEMANNI

KINGDOM OF SOISSONS

BURGUNDIANS

WESTERN ROMAN EMPIRE

KINGDOM OF ODOACER

VANDALS

BRITISH

SUEVI

VISIGOTHS

Africa

The Plates

In spite of 50 years of archaeological activity in the area inhabited by the Germanic tribes, much remains unknown or—inexcusably—unpublished. These colour plates cannot, realistically, be considered in the same light as paintings depicting later periods for which we have generous pictorial references. The surviving artefacts, and genuinely contemporary pictorial sources such as Roman triumphal sculpture, are too few; their interpretation into an integrated overall scheme is too problematical. Nevertheless, as the body of the text has shown, we *do* have more evidence than might be supposed. We believe that these plates—based upon the careful sketches prepared by the author in the course of extensive research—achieve a reasonable reconstruction of the appearance and character of these magnificent 'barbarians'.

One general thought should perhaps be recorded. In discussing the clothing of this period one often encounters phrases such as 'coarsely woven' or 'roughly made'—and these may be seriously misleading. Certainly, Roman writers make a point of the material poverty of some German tribes; but the subject and the time-scale are vast, and it is dangerous to generalise from the particular. We should be on guard against that general historical prejudice which inclines us to think of earlier peoples as, by definition, 'cruder' than ourselves. Their surviving artefacts completely disprove this, time and time again. In societies whose every need was supplied by skilled handicrafts, a mastery of tools, materials and techniques was often allied with a highly artistic instinct. The surviving Celtic weapons and armour from early in our period were made by smiths who had nothing whatever to learn from us; why should not the same be true of their womenfolk, who doubtless passed the skills of spinning and weaving down from mother to daughter as an important element in their social rôle? Why should we assume, in our bottomless arrogance, that the peoples of Iron Age Europe were any less competent at the daily tasks of their world than we are at ours?

A few precious finds of fabric clothing preserved in northern bogs suggest sturdy, long-wearing materials, sometimes with animal hair woven into the textile for added strength; but though 'coarse' in the sense of 'hairy', these fragments are by no means crudely made. The cloth is of a range of weights roughly comparable to, say, a light modern overcoat, or a heavy tweed. (It is interesting to note that modern experiments show the wool of undernourished highland sheep to be *finer* than that of fattened lowland flocks.) We have evidence of simple but pleasing decorative borders. The written descriptions of checkered patterns and stripes are supported by surviving examples of small, complex, neatly-worked 'tartans'. One such is the woman's robe from Huldre Fen, and the associated scarf; the robe is cut to fall in generous and graceful folds, and is finely sewn. The vegetable dyes used at this time probably gave quite bright colours when new, fading gradually with age into a subtle range of muted shades.

While the materials and workmanship of clothing, armour and weapons doubtless varied from region to region and from generation to generation, we should also remember that there were no rigid cultural frontiers in those days. The borders of the Empire were flexible, and porous; and a considerable trade between the Mediterranean world and the unpacified north and east of Europe continued throughout our period. Once the great migrations got under way, the mixture of styles to be seen in any one area or among any one tribal confederation must presumably have grown even more liberal.

A: Early German warriors, 1st century B.C.–1st century A.D.

The rider **A1** is mounted on a tough but probably poor-quality pony; we may infer this from the fact that the Romans, who used horsemen like this extensively, gave them better horses before training them to operate in formation. His harness is rudimentary, with few metal fittings; the 'saddle' is a folded blanket held by a sturdy leather cinch. His fringed cloak, tunic and long trousers, tied at the ankle, are all of wool. His shield is of wood covered with leather, with thin bronze edging and an iron boss, held by a central grip across the inside of the boss. Armament is limited to a light spear—*framea*—two shorter javelins, and a bronze belt-knife.

A2 and **A3** belong to one of the extensive group of Suebic tribes; their hair is dressed in the style known as the 'Suebian knot', which involved either drawing it up into a top-knot, or drawing it over to the right and knotting it above the temple. **A2** has a Celtic-type shield, whose metal boss was used offensively in combat. He is armed with a late Celtic sword of La Tène design, and a dagger; in battle he would carry several javelins, as does **A3**. This younger warrior, dressed only in a breech-clout of natural wool, carries an oval Celtic shield with a prominent central rib swelling into a boss; he might be armed with a knife in addition to his javelins.

B: Dacians, 2nd century A.D.

The chieftain, **B1**, wears a bronze helmet of Phrygian type, a corselet of iron 'leaf'-scale armour, and a black wool tunic and trousers decorated with red and white embroidery at hems and lower legs. The wool cloak, in a simple 'tartan' pattern, would probably be discarded before battle; plain colours, or a 'herringbone tweed' texture are also possible. Dacian shields shown on Trajan's Column are oval in shape, and those sculpted on the base of the column show how large and how richly decorated they were. A shield found at Pietra-Rosie in Romania, at present unpublished, bears plant motifs, and the likeness of a boar in the centre. Varieties of Dacian shields may be present on the triumphal relief from Trajan's Forum, now to be seen on the Arch of Constantine: one borne by a dismounted Praetorian trooper is oblong, with floral decoration, and a hexagonal type decorated with four Celtic carnyx trumpets and torques is seen carried by a Dacian.

The dismounted Dacian horseman, **B2**, wears a fringed cloak held by a silver ring-brooch, and natural-coloured linen tunic and trousers decorated at hem, cuffs and lower leg with red and black embroidery. His weapons are a seven-foot spear, and a long bronze La Tène sword supported by a waist belt with added bronze plates: such weapons were probably still being produced in eastern Europe by Celtic smiths. His horse would be of better quality than the pony of figure **A1**.

Two iron spearheads and an *angon***-head, found at Astwick, Bedfordshire. (British Museum)**

The Dacian tribal warrior, **B3**, wears cream-coloured trousers, sometimes decorated with bands of black embroidered patterns. The two-handed weapon is the murderous *falx*, an iron battle-scythe with the cutting edge on the inside of the curve; the *falx*, and the similar but one-handed *sica*, were the ethnic weapons of the Thracian peoples in general, and were used by part of the infantry of all Thracian groups.

C: The Marcomanni and Quadi, 1st–2nd centuries A.D.

These figures represent the most politically advanced and cohesive group of Germanic tribes of the 1st and 2nd centuries A.D. They lived in close contact with the Roman Empire and were, in consequence, exposed to strong Mediterranean influences. The chieftain, **C2**, wears a bronze helmet which appears in reasonable detail on the sculpted sarcophagus of a late Antonine general now in the Museo Nazionale delle Terme, Rome. We show it here as a Roman cavalry battle helmet mounted with a fabulous beast head to suit

47

A richly-decorated iron spearhead with bronze inlay, recovered at Great Chesterfield. (British Museum)

barbarian taste; it may, in fact, have been a cavalry sports helmet of a pattern normally equipped with a trilobate face mask, which has been removed. His mail corselet is of iron, and may have been of native manufacture; the possibility of continuing manufacture of weaponry by Celtic craftsmen in the *barbaricum* is a distinct and attractive one. The oval shield has an indent top and bottom; this pattern, and a dilobate type, seem to be peculiar to these Suebian Germans, but they also used the more common hexagonal and round patterns. The sword is of Roman origin, and has an eagle-headed pommel—there was a considerable trade in Empire-made weapons across the frontiers.

The upper-class warrior, **C3**, wears two woollen tunics, and the usual long trousers. The short sleeves of the outer tunic may have been 'notched' part way up from the hem, centrally: this feature is seen in sculptures on the sarcophagus of a Roman general who fought these tribes on the middle Danube. The hair is arranged in the 'Suebian knot', drawn over to the right temple. His weapons are a native sword on a leather baldric, and a battle-axe. Both **C2** and **C3** would have fought either mounted or on foot, as circumstances dictated.

C1 is an ordinary Suebian tribal warrior, dressed in rough woollen material with a warm jerkin of fur or fleece. He carries a javelin, a *sax*, and a shield of an old pattern, and wears amber and meerschaum beads in a double row at the neck. The cross-gartering on the legs cannot be absolutely dated to this early period; but several well-preserved corpses dating from the Celtic and Roman Iron Ages, recovered from northern European bogs, appear to wear this style— e.g. the Rendswührer Fen find of 1871. The fur shoes are

taken from a find in Fraeer Fen, Jutland—they were made of two thicknesses, the fur on the inside of the inner layer and the outside of the outer layer. In the background is a *draco* standard, a hollow bronze beast head with an attached 'windsock' of coloured fabric.

D: Gothic heavy cavalryman and infantryman, 4th century A.D.
In battle the horseman, **D1**, would have carried a long spear and a number of shorter javelins in addition to his long, 'Sarmatian' sword. His helmet, of late Roman cavalry type, is of iron with copper-gilt skinning; his mail corselet is of gilded iron, and his cloak is fastened with an iron and gilt bow-brooch. The hems and cuffs of clothing were often decorated with fur trim or embroidery; linen tunics were sometimes patterned on upper arm, neck and skirt. The round, slightly concave shield has a Roman iron boss. His mount, of about 16 hands, has iron and bronze harness fittings, and the saddle-arches are covered with stamped bronze plates, found in many Gothic burials. The infantryman, **D2**, wears two tunics, the upper one trimmed with fur; embroidery or applied cloth shapes may sometimes have been seen, in bands, simple geometric motifs, or 'dagging', to judge from Roman miniatures of the period which are thought to show Gothic influence. Shields also bore geometric shapes in primary colours. (Note that on this and some other plates we have deliberately brought such items as swords around to a slightly unconvincing angle in order to allow more visible detail.)

E: Gothic types, 4th century A.D.
The foot-soldiers, **E1** and **E3**, wear a variety of styles of woollen and linen clothing. Some probably wore tunics richly bordered with brocade or fur. This nomadic warrior people overran enemies of many groups—Slavonic, Sarmatian, Roman—and may be presumed to have profited by their success. Some tattooing of face, arms and chest is possible. Weapons ranged from bunches of javelins, and longer spears, through *saxes*, long swords and battleaxes, to bows. The bow illustrated is about 168cm long, with bronze 'nocks'; the arrows were about 90cm long, and some were tipped with armour-piercing piles. Shields were

round or oval, with iron bosses, and some probably bore geometric patterns. The unarmoured trooper, **E2**, carries a spear and a number of javelins and a long single-edged sword. Roman miniatures of the period suggest the 'dagged' tunic decoration. The oval shield, about 2ft 6ins by 3ft long, has a central arm-loop and a grip near the rim. Note particularly the wooden stirrups.

F: Frankish warriors, 5th century A.D.
Weapons particularly associated with the Franks were a javelin with a long iron shank, called an *angon* and probably derived from the Roman *pilum*; and the throwing-axe—*francisca*—with a sharply swept head. The shields have prominent bosses, either pointed, domed, or domed with a central 'button'. Note the characteristic hairstyle, with side-braids, top-knot, and the rear of the skull shaved. The writings of Sidonius Apollinaris, a 5th-century Gallo-Roman eyewitness to the Frankish invasion of Gaul, mention tunics dyed and striped in bright colours, and fur belts with inset bosses. He also mentions green cloaks bordered in red; but the scarcity of brooches in grave-finds might suggest that cloaks were not very common. Franks and Gauls enjoyed close contact for some time prior to the 5th century invasions, and it is believed that Franks would have displayed some Gallic influence in their clothing.

G: 'Anglo-Saxons', 5th century A.D.
The so-called 'Anglo-Saxon' raiders and invaders of Britain in the 4th and 5th centuries were not all Angles, Saxons and Jutes. The incoming western Germans were also represented by Frisians, Franks, and probably Alemanni; there were also a number of Wends, a Slavonic people. These figures are representative of three social divisions which were evident even as early as the writings of Tacitus in the 1st/2nd centuries. The chieftain, **G1**, is shown wearing a helmet from a later period of Saxon history—the Benty Grange find, dated to the 7th century, 200 years after the settlement of eastern Britain. It is based upon the so-called *spangenhelm*, however, and this type of composite construction was used in Europe from the 3rd right up to the 12th century, so its appearance here is not anomalous. Its iron frame originally

enclosed some kind of padded cap. The gaps in the frame are filled in with plates of split horn, giving a milky greenish-grey appearance; the helmet is held together with horn-and-hoof glue, and silver rivets in a disc-and-double-axe shape. A small silver cross or 'Thor's hammer' is mounted on the noseguard; and just forward of the apex of the skull is a small boar, decorated with four rows of gold beads and with a silver 'spat' on each quarter, mounted on a curved plate and riveted to the central iron band. The mail shirt is shown with traces of rust after a voyage—the chief's slave would doubtless spend many hours polishing it and greasing it with animal fat! The richly-decorated sword hangs from a baldric fastened by an ornate bronze buckle; in battle the warrior would also carry spears. The conical boss of the buckler was used offensively. The woollen clothing was often decorated at hem and cuffs.

The better-equipped warrior, **G2**, is a member of the chieftain's war-band. Apart from his *angon* he would carry a *francisca* and a short, single-edged sword or long knife—the *sax*. His large oval shield has a bun-shaped iron boss. He wears a 'Thor's hammer' charm on a neck-thong; and his clothing is of better quality than that of **G2**, who is an ordinary warrior/farmer, dressed in simple homespun woollens. He would normally enter battle armed with a spear as well as this one-handed battleaxe, and with a belt-knife.

H: German soldiers of the Imperial Roman Army,
*   4th–5th centuries A.D.*
H1 and **H3** are representative of the élite German regiments known as *Auxilia Palatina* (Palace Auxiliaries), raised by Constantine the Great; **H2** is a guardsman of the Emperor's German bodyguard—*Germani Corporis Custodes*—and is dressed for palace duty. In general clothing of the period seems to have been well decorated; civilian fashion inside the Empire had followed the barbarian taste for decorative embroidery and appliqué-work, and evidence for highly decorative military clothing may be found on late Roman mosaics, bas-reliefs, plates and manu-scripts. Leather belts with ornate iron fittings support long swords which invite comparison with both ancient Celtic styles and with the Roman cavalry *spatha*—with the decline in the

importance of infantry, the old legionary *gladius* had apparently given place to this type of weapon. The large oval shields seem sometimes to have had short, flighted javelins about 30cm long, with an oval lead weight on the shaft, clipped to the inner surface in some way.

Glossary

Alemanni	A confederation of German tribes who settled in Gaul.
Alans	Sarmatian nomads of south-eastern Russia.
Angles	Germans of the Baltic who took part in the settlement of the lowlands of the British mainland.
Angon	A heavy Germanic javelin.
Britons	The collective name for most of the Celts of the British mainland, some of whom settled in Gaul.
Burgundians	Germans of the middle Rhine who settled in Gaul.
Celts	A large group of Indo-Europeans.
Cimbri	A Celtic people of the middle Danube; they are believed by some scholars to be Germans.
Dacians	A Thracian people of eastern Europe, destroyed by Rome.
Foederates	Barbarians allied to Rome by treaty (*foedus*).
Francisca	The German throwing-axe used extensively by the Frankish tribes.
Franks	Germans of the Rhine who expanded into Belgium and eventually most of Gaul.
Frisians	Germans of the coastal lowlands of western Europe, some of whom took part in the settlement of Britain.
Gauls	The continental Celts.
Gepids	German people of the middle Danube; they were absorbed by the Avars, a Turco-Mongol people.
Germans	A large group of Indo-Europeans.
Goths	The most powerful group of ancient Germans. From the Baltic they spread into western Russia, eventually controlling a large part of Gaul, Italy and Spain.
Halstatt	The first Celtic Iron Age, beginning about B.C. 600.
Huns	Turco-Mongol nomads of the Eurasian plains.
Indo-Europeans	Nordic nomads of the Eurasian plains.
Iranians	A large group of Indo-European nomads.
Jutes	German people of the Baltic, who took part in the settlement of lowland Britain.

Iron Anglo-Saxon sword of the 5th to 8th century A.D. (British Museum)

La Tène	The final phase of the Celtic Iron Age beginning about B.C. 350.	
Lombards	Germanic people of northern Germany who settled in Italy.	
Marcomanni	Germans of the Danube.	
Ostrogoths	The eastern branch of the Gothic nation.	
Phrygians	A Thracian people of Asia Minor.	
Quadi	A German people of the middle Danube.	
Salian Franks	Franks of the coast of north-west Europe. 'Salty' Franks.	
Sarmatians	Iranian mounted nomads.	
Sax(Saex)	Single-edged knives common in the graves of Saxons in Britain and continental Germans.	
Saxons	Germans of the Baltic.	
Scythians	Iranian horse nomads.	
Slavs	A large group of Indo-Europeans.	
Suebi	A large group of German tribes.	
Spangenhelm	A helmet of composite construction, introduced in Europe during the 3rd century A.D.	
Teutons	A modern name for Germanic people.	
Teutones	A Celtic tribe, believed by some scholars to be Germans.	
Thracians	A large group of Indo-Europeans.	
Vandals	Germans of the Baltic who settled in Gaul, Spain and North Africa.	
Visigoths	The western branch of the Gothic people, who annexed Spain.	
Wends	A Germanized Slavonic people who took part in the German colonization of lowland Britain.	

Sources:

The plaster cast copy of Trajan's Column in the Victoria and Albert Museum, Kensington.

Trajan's Column and the Dacian Wars, Lino Rossi

The Arms and Armour of Imperial Rome, H. Russell Robinson

Oriental Armour, H. Russell Robinson

Romania, Dimitru Berciu

For those interested in further reading some books available on the subjects are listed below:

Germania, Tacitus

The Annals of Imperial Rome, Tacitus

The Histories, Tacitus

The Celts, T. G. E. Powell

The Decline and Fall of the Roman Empire, Edward Gibbon

A Study of History, Arnold Toynbee

The World of the Huns, Otto Maenchen-Halfen

The Treasure of Sutton Hoo, Bernice Groskopf

The Age of Arthur, John Morris

The Anglo-Saxons, D. J. V. Fisher

Anglo-Saxon England, Sir Frank Stenton

Roman Britain and the English Settlements, R. G. Collingswood & J. N. L. Myers

Arthur's Britain, L. Alcock

Races of Europe, by Carleton S. Coon

The World of Late Antiquity, P. Brown

The Kingdom of the Franks, P. Lasko

The Barbarian West, J. M. Wallace-Hadrill

The Northern Barbarians, M. Todd

The Penguin Atlas of Ancient History, Colin McEvedy

The Penguin Atlas of Medieval History, Colin McEvedy

Archaeology of Weapons, Ewart Oakeshott

Dark Age Warrior, Ewart Oakeshott

The Dark Ages, edited by David Talbot Rice

The Goths in Spain, E. A. Thompson

Barbarian Europe, Philip Dixon

The Art of War in the Middle Ages, Sir Charles Oman

The Bog People, P. V. Glob

The Vikings and Their Origins, D. Wilson

The Slavs, M. Gimbutas

The Armies and Enemies of Imperial Rome, Phil Barker

Armies of the Dark Ages 600–1066, Ian Heath

Rome's Enemies: Gallic and British Celts

Chronology

3000 BC Nomadic Indo-European warriors begin to colonise large areas of Europe, settling among New Stone Age farmers and Old Stone Age hunters in the north.

1800 BC Proto-Celts begin moving into western Europe.

1600 BC Proto-Celts dominate the British Isles and the Atlantic coast of Iberia.

1200 BC A new Celtic culture evolves, named after the fields of individual cremation urns corresponding to areas of Celtic settlement in middle Europe.

1000 BC The 'Urnfield' culture spreads into most of France at the expense of the earlier 'Tumulus' culture of the Proto-Celts.

800 BC 'Urnfield' Celts begin expansion into the Iberian peninsula. Scythians penetrate Europe. The Illyrian Halstatt culture begins.

670 BC The Iberians of Eastern Spain are overrun by 'Urnfield' Celts. Iron working is in progress in the Celtic regions of the Danube. Iron weapons appear in the Celtic waggon graves of Bohemia and southern Germany.

600 BC The Iron Age Halstatt culture emerges among the Celts of Central Europe. The Celts of Spain penetrate the central Iberian plateau. The Iberians regain independence in the north and east, thus dislocating the trans-Pyrenean link between the Celts of Spain and Gaul. Celtic trade increases with the Greeks and Etruscans.

500 BC Halstatt Celts begin to move into mainland Britain.

400 BC The Iron Age La Tène culture begins its first phase. La Tène Celts become known to ancient writers, who call them Gauls. The Gauls cross the Alps, flooding into the valley of the Po. Northern Etruscan communities are expunged. Latium is invaded and Rome sacked.

368 BC Gallic mercenaries are employed in the army of Syracuse.

341 BC Roman defeat of the Gauls in Latium.

285 BC Roman conquest of the Ager Gallicus.

Bronze dagger hilt and scabbard of unknown provenance, but dating from the late Halstatt period—the 6th century BC.

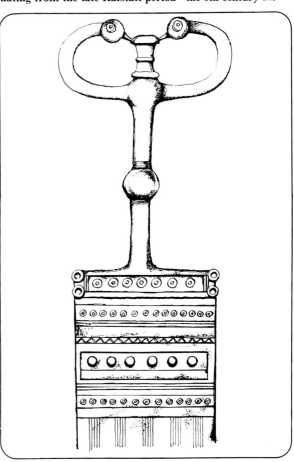

Northern European Bronze Age warrior's burial clothing, found perfectly preserved in an oak coffin. The material is wool mixed with hart's hair. The bronze sword is from an oak coffin at Borum Eshoj; carried in a wooden scabbard, it was suspended from a long baldric which would have allowed the weapon to drag along the ground if not supported. These burials, the so-called 'Mound Warriors', were from an intrusive warlike group which reached Denmark; they probably included proto-Celtic chieftains.

	expansion begins to wane. La Tène Celts (Gauls) begin to move into Britain. Many Gauls in Carthaginian service.
218 BC	Celts involved as allies of Carthage during the Second Punic War. Their power in Italy declines.
125 BC	Roman conquest of southern Gaul.
118 BC	The Cimbri, a Celtic tribe from the middle Danube, attack Noricum.
113 BC	War between Rome and Celto-Spaniards ('Celtiberians').
105 BC	Cimbri and Teutones defeat Roman forces at Orange.
102–1 BC	Roman forces destroy the Cimbri and Teutones.
100 BC	Belgic Gauls begin migration to southern Britain.
58 BC	The beginning of the final subjugation of Gaul.
55–4 BC	Roman forces probe southern Britain.
52 BC	Vercingetorix leads a major Gallic rebellion, which is defeated by Caesar at Alesia.
AD 9	Northern German tribes annihilate three Roman legions in the Teutoburg Forest.
AD 43	Roman invasion of southern Britain.
AD 61	British revolt led by Boudicca, Queen of the Iceni.
AD 69	The Romanisation of southern Britain is completed.
AD 84	Roman forces defeat the Caledonians in northern Britain.

279 BC	Beginning of an insular La Tène art style in Britain. Gauls invade Macedon, Greece and Thrace. Three tribes cross the Hellespont into central Anatolia, which becomes Galatia.
274 BC	Gallic warriors in Greek, Egyptian and other armies of the near East.
264–241 BC	Celtic warriors involved in the First Punic War.
240 BC	Attalos defeats the Gauls ('Galatians') of Asia Minor.
225 BC	The Gauls of the Po Valley and Trans-Alpine élite warriors are defeated at Telamon, Tuscany. Gallic

Introduction

The military ascendancy of the Celtic warrior north of the Alps was brought to an end when the loosely-knit Celtic 'empire', established in a great anarchic band across central Europe from the Atlantic coasts of the British Isles to the Black Sea, collapsed piecemeal in the face of the relentless campaigns of Julius Caesar.

Successive waves of warlike Indo-European tribes had by about 1000 BC given most of Europe an overlay of warrior-farmers. Hellenic tribes had

colonised Greece. Thracians had moved into areas north of Greece; Italic and Celtic tribes were in Italy; Celts were in the British Isles, Spain and central Europe; Teutons were occupying most of Scandinavia and the north-western coastlands of Europe, with the Slavs and Balts on their north-eastern flank.

At about this time the 'Urnfield' Celts began an expansion to the west from the region of the upper Danube. In around 800 BC the 'Urnfielders' had also spread east on to the Hungarian *puszta* and to the south-west, where they stood at the gates of Spain. During the early 8th century BC they had crossed the eastern passes of the Pyrenees and had occupied a wide inland area with the Mediterranean coast on their left flank.

At the beginning of the 6th century BC 'Urnfield' Celts were involved in the Illyrian Iron Age culture named by modern archaeologists after the first find-spot of the extensive cemetery which had belonged to a wealthy salt mining community: Halstatt, a village near Salzburg, Austria is on a lakeside where the original excavations took place in the 19th century.

Most of our knowledge of early Celtic culture is based on the rich finds from the early burials in Bavaria, Bohemia and Upper Austria. These princely tombs contained a waggon, or its dismembered parts, on which the corpse was laid together with an iron sword and spears, an ample supply of pottery, sometimes cauldrons, and joints of beef and pork. Some graves also contained yokes, harness and bronze bits for the two waggon horses, and a third set probably for a riding horse. The whole tomb was usually encased in an oblong wooden chamber beneath an earthen mound or barrow.

Towards the end of the 'Halstatt period' the funeral vehicle became a two-wheeled chariot. The important centres in which these inhumations are found show a strong tendency to be sited further to the west the later they are, which most probably indicates the general drift west of a 'Royal' group of

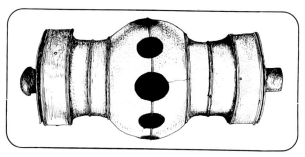

Bronze shell from one of the hub-blocks of a four-wheeled waggon burial at Viz, Burgundy dating from the 5th century BC. A relatively sophisticated casting like this, for a piece of utilitarian vehicle equipment, indicates a high level of technical skill. It is finds like this, at first sight much less dramatic than weapons or jewellery, which remind us that the Celts were very far from being the savages patronised by some Classical writers.

La Tène expansion from the old Halstatt Celtic areas in central Europe and Britain, about 200 BC; the speckled areas indicate Urnfield Celtic territories.

Celtic warriors. By the 3rd century BC, warriors buried in this manner had arrived in Britain.

The Gauls made their entry with the advent of the 'La Tène' culture in Celtic territory. The Celts knew themselves as Celtae; the Greeks knew them as Keltoi, the Romans called them Galli or Galatae, but recognised that all these terms were interchangeable. To earlier Greek writers the Celts and Germans were grouped together as 'unmounted Scythians'. It is with the Roman version, the Galli (Gauls), that most 'La Tène' Celts are associated.

The first Celtic La Tène Iron Age phase roughly corresponds with a widespread avalanche of Gauls into Italy, Eastern Europe, France, Denmark and the British Isles. Gallic settlement of northern Italy centred on the Upper Po Valley and those of its

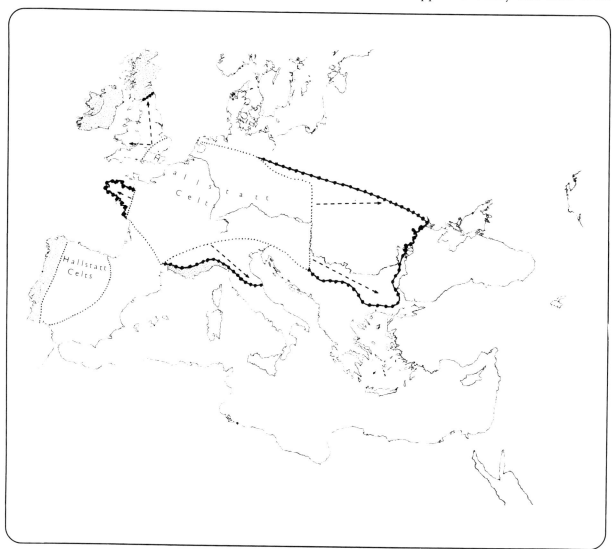

tributaries. They poured through Alpine passes, obliterating the infrastructure of northern Etruscan society; long-standing trade contracts between the Gauls and Etruscans would have made it obvious to the Gauls that Etruscan society had begun to show some signs of disintegration at this time.

The declared origins of these invaders are confirmed by archaeology as being Switzerland and southern Germany. The tribes who had traversed the central Alpine massif are recorded as being led by the Insubres, who settled around Mediolanum, now Milan. They were followed by the Laii, Libici, Cenomani and Anari who settled in Lombardy. Later waves included the Boii and Lingones who passed through the new Gallic territories finding their own area in Emelia. Last to arrive were the Senones, who settled the poorer land along the Adriatic coast of Umbria.

Swiftly-moving, marauding bands of unencumbered warriors raided deeper into the peninsula. The main armies and caravans of family waggons followed, stopping at the main areas of settlement. Roman influence in southern Etruria was temporarily disrupted by the Gallic incursions, but during the ensuing chaos Rome destroyed Etruscan power and influence among her Italic allies. The Etruscans, though not lacking valour, never developed a successful enough technique for dealing with Gallic warriors and their northern citizens began settling further to the south. Etruscan culture and history were eventually to be absorbed by the nascent and vigorous Roman Republican state to the south.

In 390 BC a meeting between a Roman embassy of three patrician delegates and the Senones took place at the Etruscan town of Clusium; the Romans were invited by the anxious burghers of the town to mediate with the barbarians. During an ensuing dispute one of the Gallic leaders received a fatal wound, and the Roman party made an immediate and hurried departure. There followed a demand from the Gauls for all three patricians to be returned for retribution. The Roman authorities refused, and awaited barbarian reaction, confident in their ability to deal with it. The Gauls promptly wrenched their standards from the ground and marched south.

The Roman army of about 15,000 men sent to bar the way to Rome was destroyed, 11 miles north

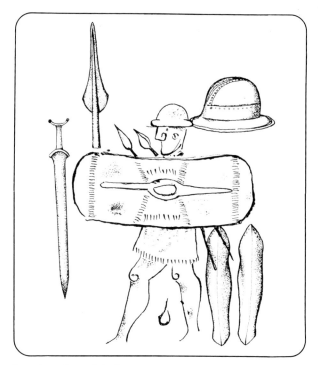

Drawing of one of the figures embossed on the surface of a 5th-century BC bronze bucket from Certosa, northern Italy. There is a strong likelihood that he represents a Celtic warrior: his shield is of Celtic type, and this shape of helmet was common in Celtic areas of northern Italy and south and central Europe. He is surrounded here by drawings of arms and armour from a late Halstatt chariot burial at Cesto Calende, northern Italy, dating from the 6th century: an iron antennae sword found in a bronze scabbard, an iron spearhead, bronze greaves, and a wide-brimmed bronze helmet with a crest slot.

of the city, at the confluence of the Rivers Allia and Tiber. Three days after the battle the Gauls entered Rome, much of which they burnt. Senators were slaughtered in the Senate House. Many citizens were saved by cackling geese giving the alarm during a Gallic night attack on the Capitol where they had sought sanctuary. The barbarians demanded a huge bounty of gold to leave the city. During the weighing procedure, Brennus, the Gallic leader, is said to have thrown his sword on to the scales with the words 'Vae victis'—'Woe to the defeated'.

Without doubt, the capture, occupation and sack of the city remained an indelible mark on Roman folk memory. We can only guess how great a part it played in Rome's merciless treatment of the Celts in subsequent wars. Repeatedly beaten in battle, the Celts were subjected to wholesale massacres which almost merit that overworked word, 'genocide'. This implacable hostility did not ease until Gauls and Britons were finally incorporated into the

Roman Empire. (It should be noted, nevertheless, that large numbers of Celts were accepted into the Roman army from the earliest opportunity.)

The Celts possessed many impressive qualities; and in the 4th century the writer Ephorus named the Celts, Persians, Scythians and Lybians as the four great barbarian peoples of the known world. Celtic technical skills, particularly their artistry in metalwork, were of the very highest calibre; and are matched, in surviving artefacts, by an abstract artistic vision which can be breathtaking in its beauty. They loved display—display of material wealth and beauty, as in the colourful clothing and collars and armlets of precious metals which bedecked their chiefs and warriors; and display of human qualities, as in their bragging of ancestry, strength and prowess. They bellowed insult and challenge across the battle-lines. At their great feasts they were quick to laughter, and to ferocity. Their spirits could be moved quickly from deep troughs of melancholy to furious outbursts of uncontrolled energy.

Arms from the tomb of a Celtic warrior found in Romania, dating from the 3rd century BC: bronze helmet, iron spearheads, iron sword in a bronze scabbard, iron dagger in a bronze scabbard, iron 'sabre'. The sword has been deliberately 'killed'—folded in two—before burial.

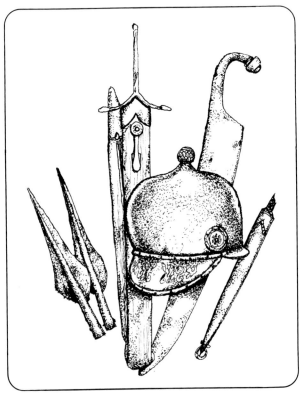

Astonishing examples of loyalty unto death went hand in hand with tales of appalling treacheries. Blood-feuds were commonplace; and the cult of head-hunting played a major part in their feelings about war and the supernatural. They were a people capable of fine gold-work of the utmost subtlety; of enamelled brooches, utensils and weapons of nearly unequalled quality—and yet a people whose dark beliefs allowed them to commit unspeakable acts of savagery against helpless captives. They were a contradictory, tumultuous, dynamic, and infinitely spectacular people, whose blood is permanently mixed into that of the inhabitants of the British Isles and north-west Europe.

The Warrior

Many authorities are of the opinion that Celtic expansion did not involve a special racial type, and that the descriptive use of the word 'Celtic' is only valid as a linguistic term. Others believe that ample skeletal remains contradict this view, since all Celtic remains show the same Nordic characteristics as their descendants.

The unforgettable appearance to southern European eyes of Celtic warriors—their height, white skin, muscularity, fair hair and blue eyes—points to a particularly heavy concentration of these physical characteristics among the warrior class, descendants of the intrusive Indo-European warrior-farmers of an earlier age. The paramount function of this warrior caste was precisely that of appearing on battlefields, opposing all kinds of southern Europeans or any other challengers to Celtic arms. To most outsiders, the Celts would all be assumed to be of this particular type. It is logical to assume that this blonde warrior caste represented the 'Celts proper'; and Classical sculpture, mainly from the Pergamene school, confirms the literary descriptions of their tall, athletic, muscular bodies and wavy or curly hair.

This abundant hair was left uncut by most warriors. In some cases it was plaited so as to hang on either side of the forehead. The Sicilian-Greek Diodorus describes how some Celts smeared their hair with a thick lime wash and drew it back from

Two 2nd-century BC electrum torcs from Ipswich, England. These gold alloy neck rings are made from two rods twisted together and thickened at the ends, which bear La Tène floral curvilinear designs. (British Museum)

the forehead to produce a weird effect, like the flying white mane of a horse. Drooping moustaches were popular. Bearded warriors are shown on the Arch of Orange.

The Celtic Iron Age fashion of wearing trousers was particularly noted by Greek and Roman writers. Diodorus Siculus, probably quoting the Syrian historian Posidonius, writes of the colourful clothing worn by the Gauls, as well as their use of trousers; the 'multi-coloured' fabric associated with the Celts probably indicates checkered and striped patterns, but they also wore fabrics of solid colours, natural wool colours and linen. Tunics with long or short sleeves were worn with a waist belt or girdle; over this was worn a cloak. Braiding and fringes were attached separately. Leather shoes completed the turnout.

Neck rings, known as torcs, were worn by chieftains and many warriors, made of gold, electrum, silver and bronze. Most surviving examples are of exquisite workmanship. They were worn by the Celts from about the 5th century BC; the finest examples of metallic Celtic jewellery belong to this early La Tène phase. Classical sculpture and native art distinctly show Celtic warriors wearing these torcs. They are also shown on Roman military funerary stones, together with other decorative awards on chest harness worn by centurions. Large numbers of these torcs must have

fallen into the hands of victorious Roman forces in their wars with the Gauls; perhaps more significant is the Romans' copying of this and other fashions from their deadly but impressive enemies.

Bronze brooches, often embellished with studs mounted with coral or exquisitely enamelled, are found in warrior graves singly or in pairs, in the region of the chest where they had held a cloak in place.

Roman fear of the awesome and dangerous Celtic charge was eventually overcome when it was realised that steadiness, thorough battle training, the use of ample reserves and, above all, a complete range of missiles could usually be relied upon to defeat even the most determined avalanche of battle crazed Gallic savages.

One of the best insights into the character of the Celtic warrior was written by Strabo, a Greek geographer who lived around the beginning of the 1st century AD. He wrote: 'The whole race, which is now called Celtic or Galatic, is madly fond of war, high spirited and quick to battle, but otherwise straightforward and not of evil character. And so when they are stirred up they assemble in their bands for battle, quite openly and without

Small bronze, found near Rome and dated to the 3rd century BC, which depicts a naked Gaulish warrior as described by Classical writers. He is either casting a javelin or defending himself with a sword; the shield, which would have been fixed to his left arm, is missing. The horned helmet is not recognisably Celtic, but the large torc and plated belt are well defined. Naked 'Gaesatae' like this man fought at the battle of Telamon in 225 BC; these 'Spear-wielders' from north of the Alps enjoyed a special status. (Staatliche Museen zu Berlin)

forethought; so that they are easily handled by those who desire to outwit them. For at any time or place, and on whatever pretext you stir them up, you will have them ready to face danger, even if they have nothing on their side but their own strength and courage. . . . To the frankness and high-spiritedness of their temperament must be added the traits of childish boastfulness and love of decoration. . . .'

Caesar wrote that Gaulish society was divided into three classes: *druides* or priests, *equites* or 'knights', and *plebs* or common people. The tie of personal clientship between a Gallic noble and his retainers operated to the mutual advantage of both. The more retainers and clients a noble could acquire, the greater his local influence and the stability of his power.

From early puberty the young man of the warrior caste progressed through the martial arts of the Celt, with the accompaniment of hunting, feasting and drinking. As a fully-fledged warrior he would support and be supported in battle by a close age group of his own peers, who had been with him throughout his training for manhood. In this way many young men developed a strong man-to-man bond; and Diodorus, Strabo and Athenaeus all remark that homo-erotic practices were accepted among Celtic warriors.

Celtic communities: fort and farmstead

Since the Celts left no written record, our only knowledge of the arrangement of their lives and their communities comes from the brief, and perhaps unreliable accounts left by Roman writers, and from the evidence of the spade. There are few clues to any detailed understanding of their society. We know that they were a 'tribal' people; we do not know exactly what their tribal structure was. We are told that they were a society divided by caste into a warrior 'aristocracy', a priestly class, and an underclass of peasants. We know that they practised slavery.

As for their pattern of building, the modern academic view is that a fairly highly organised society of scattered farms and farming hamlets looked towards local 'hill forts' as the focus of their lives. These 'forts' present a bewildering range of size, local density, and apparent purpose. Some are only an acre or two in extent, with a simple rampart-and-ditch defence, and traces of a handful of huts. Others enclose within huge multiple rampart systems scores or even hundreds of acres, and traces of up to several hundred huts. There are examples which fall at every point along this range of size. Some may have been villages; some were almost certainly simply refuges for people and their beasts in time of war; and the largest and most densely built-up can only be described as 'towns'— perhaps even as local 'capitals'. We simply do not know how Celtic 'political' society worked; so we cannot make intelligent guesses about the comparative frequency of purely military 'forts', fortified refuges, permanent fortified villages, or massively defended 'royal capitals'.

One safe assumption is that the time-smoothed banks and faint traces of post-holes, which today crown almost every skyline in some parts of Britain and continental Europe, give an altogether too primitive impression. The archaeological evidence shows a wide range of construction techniques, some extremely sophisticated. Ramparts which even today survive to a height of 90 feet would then have been much more sharply sloped and sculpted. Some were built up by means of timber lacing, rubble in-fill, and vertical facing walls of dry stone

Helmets from the triumphal arch at Orange—ancient Arausio—in Vaucluse, southern France. The Orange bas-reliefs show masses of Gallic arms and military trumpets. The helmets are crested with a wheel, the Celtic symbol of war. Some authorities believe them to be ceremonial helmets, but they could equally be battle pieces. They may represent late survivals of 'Montefortino' helmets.

blocks. Some had defended gateways with indirect approaches and outworks which are reminiscent in their sound design of 18th century forts. We find evidence for massive timber gates surmounted by patrol-walks; for multiple stone-faced ramparts, quite possibly spaced according to the effective range of the available missile weapons; for a hierarchy wielding enough authority to stockpile 50,000 large sling-stones in handy positions on the ramparts of a fort, after gathering them from a beach some miles away. Whatever our ignorance of these people, one thing is sure: their chieftains had real authority, and wielded it over a social system wealthy and organised enough to put considerable manpower at their disposal for sustained tasks.

Julius Caesar describes encountering in central and northern Gaul a type of solid defensive wall which he terms *murus Gallicus*. This can best be described as a skeletal grid of timber beams placed crossways and nailed together, built up in layers, with earth and rubble rammed down into the spaces between the beams at every level. A dry stone wall faced this construction front and back— sometimes covering the ends of the lateral beams, sometimes leaving them exposed. The core of the wall thus gave good resistance to battering rams, even when the facing had been breached; and the facing and in-fill protected the timber skeleton from fire. This 'Gallic wall' is known to have been at least 12 ft high in some cases.

The Gallic Celts came in contact with Greek settlers in southern France, and it is tantalising to wonder how much this contact affected Celtic defensive engineering. In this area several strong-holds have been identified which boasted ram-parts of stone construction, rather than of stone-faced earth. The best-known is Entremont, which the Romans described as an *oppidum*—'town'. Overlooking Aix-en-Provence, this triangular fort-ress, captured by the Romans in 123 BC, had walls of rough-cut stone blocks defended at intervals of about every 20 yards by towers with solid rubble-packed bases; the walls probably boasted battle-ments or parapets originally. Britain has not

produced evidence of comparable sophistication. There are signs that some British forts were given improved defences at several periods; in about the 3rd century BC there was a general deepening of ditches and heightening of ramparts, and on some southern British sites the 1st century BC saw the raising of additional belts of ramparts and ditches and the construction of sophisticated indirect entranceways.

The settlements which were scattered right across the Celts' geographical range offer just as wide a variety of sizes and designs as the 'forts', from isolated farmsteads perhaps supporting one extended family, to quite large villages of up to 40 acres or so—larger than most medieval and many modern villages. There have been several recent experiments in reconstructing, from archaeological evidence, working Iron Age farmsteads. A project on Butser Hill near Petersfield, Hampshire included several different types of living units based on post-hole measurements and surviving fragments of hut fabric. In fields cultivated by hand, or with primitive ploughs drawn by cattle, experimental crops of cereals thought to resemble contemporary grains have been raised. Crops such as spelt and emma were found to average some 1,600 lbs yield per acre even in poor conditions. Breeds of horse, cow, poultry and sheep which approximate ancient strains have been raised on these experimental farms—for instance the agile and hardy St Kilda sheep, a small goat-like creature raised for its wool. Weaving, potting, charcoal-burning and metal-smelting—all necessary to a Celtic community—have been practised on these sites using the reconstructed technology of the period. In the lower strata of Celtic society most men, women and children would have spent the bulk of their lives carrying out these labour-intensive tasks.

Exterior and interior views of the Iron Age 'Pimperne house' (named after the site of an important archaeological find) which was carefully reconstructed at Butser Hill near Petersfield, Hampshire as part of an experimental recreation of a working farmstead of the Celtic period. These photographs remind us that the phrase 'thatched hut' can be misleading: this is a large, solidly-constructed dwelling of sturdy appearance. We have no idea what the interior arrangements or furnishings were like, since archaeologists have little more than post holes and the traces of hearths to go by. Experience suggests that it is probably a mistake to assume primitive squalor. (Richard Muir)

The Druids

The ancient Celts were not a religious people, in the sense of worshipping an established hierarchy of gods. But they were intensely superstitious; they believed that the objects and the environment of their physical world were pervaded by magical agencies. Placation by ritual and sacrifice—including, according to the Romans, human sacrifice—and by the telling of sacred myths and tales was believed to encourage benign involvement by supernatural powers in human affairs. The Celtic year was punctuated by festivals marking the farming seasons.

There was no organised pantheon of gods such as that of the Greeks and Romans, although much of the terminology attributed to the Celts (or perhaps simply 'filtered through' the Graeco-Roman vocabulary of the commentators) seems common to most Indo-European peoples. Some Celtic deities were of only local importance; others were 'national' gods. Some were believed capable of shape-changing, from human to bird or animal form.

Their sacred places, with the exception of sanctuaries such as Roquepertuse and Entremont, were evidently simple groves or woods. Ceremonies were conducted here by the priestly class, or 'druids'. Pliny mentions the connection between druidic rites and oak trees. Mistletoe was ritually cut from oak trees, usually accompanied by a bull sacrifice; but the purpose of the custom is obscure.

Caesar notes the importance of the druids in Gaul both as magicians and as arbitrators to whom disputes or problems were taken. They seem to have been the guardians of the Celts' oral traditions, through ritual myths passed from generation to generation. In short, they were 'witch doctors' or 'wise men', whose influence was woven deeply and intricately into Celtic life. Britain had a particularly strong reputation as a cradle of druids, and this was apparently more than simply the result of druids fleeing to Britain after the fall of Gaul to the Romans. The Roman invaders were implacably hostile to the druidic cult, and their writers make much of the inhuman sacrificial customs they sometimes practised. One may suppose that just as important to the invaders was the need to stamp out ruthlessly this network or 'infrastructure' for preserving Celtic national consciousness right across tribal divisions. The last and most influential centre of open, 'organised' druidism was in the west of Britain, where the stronghold of the cult on the island of Anglesey was destroyed by Suetonius Paulinus in AD 60.

Head-hunting

In a man's head lay his mind, his strength, his will, his spirit, his 'life force'. The American Indian believed that to remain in the domestic environment of the camp, surrounded by women, children, and the smells of cooking and the camp fire was to become softened and weak; while to live in the fresh air, to kill enemy warriors and to take into one's being their manly strength and spirit, was to become oneself a powerful warrior. Some such feeling as this probably lay behind the Celtic cult of head-collecting; but its symbols are so pervasive in surviving Celtic art and artefacts that we may suspect a developed and deeply-held system of belief, even if we cannot identify it in detail. The image of the severed head is found everywhere—in carved stone and wooden objects, and in the form of actual surviving skulls. Heads were placed on

Helmets of 'Coolus' type, as first discovered in that district of the Marne. These simple helmets are of the true 'reversed jockey cap' shape. Those marked here A and B are Roman adaptations of the design, with two rivet holes on each side to attach cheek guards. The original Celtic examples have only one hole each side for a simple chin strap. The rings fitted under the neck guard may have been a third attachment point for the chin straps, or simply carrying lugs. (From various sources)

gateway lintels; in niches in temples, or in the door-beams of buildings; even collected and kept inside huts. Some very prized heads were kept embalmed in cedar oil in special chests. When freshly taken the head was hung by the hair from a warrior's spear, chariot, or horse's harness.

Weapon sacrifice

Orosius, a Roman historian, leaves this comment on the ritual destruction of booty by the Cimbri after the battle of Arausio in 105 BC: 'When the enemy had taken possession of two camps and an immense booty, they destroyed under new and strange oaths and imprecations all that had fallen into their hands. . . .'

A later witness to this custom was Caesar, who wrote of the Gauls: 'When they have decided to fight a battle they generally vow to Mars the booty they hope to take, and after a victory they sacrifice the captured animals and collect the rest of the spoil in one spot. Among many of the tribes, high piles of it can be seen on consecrated ground.' These votive deposits, dedicated to a god by the victors in inter-tribal wars, are found in different locations all over Europe where the Celts held sway. From pools, lakes, marshes and peat-bogs the remains of excellent swords, spears, daggers, mail, chariot wheels, shields, trumpets, and large deposits of animal bones have all been brought to light—indeed, it is from them that historians have learned most about Celtic war-gear.

Arms and Armour

The incredible impression made by Celtic warriors on those southern Europeans who came into contact with them is registered in literature, surviving sculpture and the minor arts.

Prior to the 3rd century BC the Celts used very little armour, many warriors choosing to fight naked. Chieftains and the wealthier warriors did wear helmets and body armour to a greater degree as contact with southern armies became more frequent. This trend increasingly spread down to the lower strata. Several graves in northern Italy contain Etruscan armour and Celtic weapons; some experts believe, however, that these are probably not Celtic because of the presence of a Greek heavy infantry shield (*hoplon*) in one of this series of burials.

Southern Europeans never thought of the Celt particularly as an armoured warrior; even after long involvement with the sophisticated armies of Rome, the majority of Gauls wore no body defences. Ironically, some of the battle helmet types used by Roman armies are, in Russell Robinson's view, direct developments of Gallic originals.

Montefortino and Coolus helmets

The helmets used by more northerly Gauls at the beginning of the La Tène period (during the late 5th century BC) are varied in design. Some are of a graceful conical shape, sometimes with quite a steep apex which was completed with a hollow finial; others are of a 'reversed plain jockey cap' shape. Later Gallic helmets show their descent from these earlier examples. Named after the necropolis at Montefortino, Ancona in northern Italy, the Montefortino type 'jockey cap' helmet was made of bronze or, more rarely, iron. Other 'jockey cap' Celtic helmets were found in the Coolus district of the Marne in north-eastern France. Most were of bronze.

The Montefortino 'jockey cap' evolved about the beginning of the 4th century BC, the finest examples of these beautiful headpieces being found in Italy although they originated in barbarian Europe. They were to prove extremely popular throughout both Roman and Carthaginian armies. When later versions were mass produced, their quality deteriorated. The helmet was held in place by

straps which ran from the neck guard, where they were attached, to metal loops, hooks or studs on the lower part of each cheek guard. Crests were of several types, known examples having several knobs at the apex, metallic branches from a central insert, and hollow finials to accept feather or flowing horsehair plumes. The helmet shell was sometimes fitted with slots or pockets for flat metal 'horns' to be slid into place on either side of the skull.

The Coolus 'jockey cap' has a flat guard projecting horizontally from the back of the lower shell, as a neck guard. These metal caps were of a simple, utilitarian, hemispherical design with no crest fittings. They date from the 3rd to the 1st century BC, and in all probability were manufactured by Celtic armourers for the Roman army during and after the conquest. Many surviving Roman army helmets of Coolus type in a developed form have crest attachments and cheek guards.

Agen helmets

So far four late Gallic brimmed iron helmets have come to light; they are named after the find-spot of the first of the small series found at Agen, Lot-et-Garonne, Switzerland. They have deep, full shells, not unlike a bowler hat, with a wide brim at the lower edge, narrow in the front and wide at the back, the neck guard section being stepped to reinforce it. A further raised V-sectioned reinforcement encircles the wall of the shell. The cheek guards are mounted with curvilinear embossing, patterned bosses and stepping. The headpiece was secured by thongs through the rings at the underside of the neck guard and the lower rear corners of the cheek guards.

Port helmets

Named after Port Bei Nidau, in Switzerland, where the first of this series was found, these Gallic iron helmets of Port type have deep shells like the Agen helmets. The forward rim is extended into a small peak; the rear of the shell is continued down to lower ear level. This neck guard has two ridges across its width, and the lower edge is brought out to a narrow horizontal stop. The shell front has two raised ridges above the forehead forming two recurved 'eyebrows' almost meeting in the middle, where a large rivet forms a small boss.

Fragments of both types of the late Gallic helmets

1st-century BC bronze helmet with a central reinforcement mounted with two triple finials on the crown, and a duck or goose head at the front. Of great interest are the fabric inner cap, and the fabric-lined leather cheek guards; this type of non-metallic fitting almost never survives. The band around the edge of the skull is embossed with a simple repeat pattern of 'double hooks'. (Schweiz Landesmuseum, Zurich)

An iron helmet of the 'Agen/Port' type dating from the 1st century BC. It has a deep, vertical-sided skull and a narrow brim broadening into a neck guard at the back; this had two reversed cusps at each side, and a 'stepped' surface for added strength. From Giubasco, Ticino. (Schweiz Landesmuseum, Zurich)

were found at Alesia, where a Gallic force led by Vercingetorix was trapped during a siege in 52 BC. In the opinion of the late Russell Robinson, these Agen/Port helmets were the direct ancestors of the Imperial Gallic Roman battle helmets of later centuries.

Helmets of exotic type were also acquired by the Gauls from the earliest times, including Greek varieties, Italo-Corinthian, Italo-Attic and Etruscan Negau types.

Helmet linings

In his book on Roman Imperial armour, the late Russell Robinson mentions a quantity of surviving linings in helmets of the 14th to 17th centuries AD. The majority are made up of four segments, some of more, their upper ends joined by a circling lace which could be adjusted to enable the helmet to seat on the head at the correct height. This method is still used in modern helmets of all kinds. In all cases the linings are fastened to the helmet rim, and have a space between the top of the helmet and upper lining, in order to eliminate condensation and allow free circulation of air. A padded fabric of hard-wearing type is usual. In view of the known longevity of this method of helmet lining, there is no reason to doubt that earlier fittings of this type were used in the helmets of both Gauls and Romans. A cheek guard found at Hod Hill, Dorset has traces of fabric on its inside surface, which would seem to be the remains of a lining of simple padded type which was either stuck on or secured under the edge-binding. There is also some evidence that some form of arming cap was in use during centuries prior to the Middle Ages.

Armour

Body armour was always much rarer among the Celts than helmets. Some Celts of the Urnfield culture were equipped with bronze plate armour which included cuirasses and greaves; production skills were probably derived from Mycenaean craftsmen, and the earliest examples from eastern Europe date to the 13th century BC. Some examples are heavily embossed and incised. The earliest representations of mail are on the reliefs of the temple of Athene at Pergamon in Turkey; they are included in the frieze showing captured arms and armour of the Galatians. The mail is shown made up into sleeveless shirts with reinforcement panels for the shoulders attached across the top of the back and held at the front by a bar and stud device. Dated to the early 2nd century BC, the frieze probably shows examples of the captured equipment copied on site by the sculptor.

A more developed form of this type of mail corselet was used by Roman, Etruscan and later Gallic warriors. A clearly illustrated example of this

The young Gallic nobleman of Vachères, Basses Alpes, discovered in 1892; this probably represents one of the class of *equites* or 'knights' described by Caesar. The mail corselet, with its shoulder reinforcements, is clearly defined. The cuffed tunic is split at each side of the hem. (Musée Calvet, Avignon)

Detail of the sword, belt, and cuffed sleeve of the Vachères warrior. (Musée Calvet, Avignon)

Gallic armours are found on the remains of statues and figurines from southern France and northern Italy. They are in the form of a shawl or cape, which is joined at the two upper corners of each end by hook-and-plate attachments at the centre of the upper chest. Most examples show angled ends on the chest, but others are rounded off.

The Celtic shield

For the majority of Gaulish warriors the shield was important as their only defence, crucial to their fighting technique.

The earliest Celtic shields were relatively small 'targets' of hide or wood. If the round 'parade' shields of thin bronze found in central Europe, Greece and Italy can be taken as samples of the appearance of contemporary and earlier battle shields of this type, they were heavily studded.

At some time during the Halstatt cultural period the Celts adopted the long body shield. Most probably developed from Italic prototypes, the long Celtic shield was oblong, shaped either as a hexagon or as a complete or truncated oval. Examples of early Celtic long shields are most probably shown on a bronze bucket from northern Italy where we see warriors in brimmed 'bowler hat' helmets carrying two spears and long, round-cornered, oblong shields with a central spine and oblong boss.

Remains of long Celtic shields have been discovered at La Tène in France, Hjortspring in Denmark, and in Ireland. The La Tène examples were originally oval and about 1.1 metre long; they are made of oak planks which were chamfered to a thinner section towards the rim. The centre was reinforced by a wooden spine, swelling in the middle, which was hollowed out to correspond with a round or oval cut-out in the shield centre. The hollow was usually protected by a bronze or iron strap-type boss which crossed over the wide section of the spine and was riveted through the shield. The hand grip was fashioned in wood, sometimes reinforced with a metal strap riveted on either side of the hollow through the shield. The flat area of the face and back of the shield was covered with leather, or sometimes perhaps with felt. An extra metal binding or 'piping' was applied to the upper rim of some shields to guard against downward strokes of sword or axe, which could split the wood.

Variations of this basic shield type are to be seen

armour is to be seen worn by the aristocratic young Gallic warrior whose statue was found at Vachères in southern France. The young man rests his left arm on the top of his long shield. He is dressed in a long-sleeved tunic with turn-back cuffs, and a cloak caught with a brooch on the right shoulder. A large plain torc surrounds his neck. The mail corselet consists of a shirt with short sleeves just covering the shoulder angle. The oblong shoulder reinforcements are attached across the top of the back and are held in place below the pectorals with large studs. A double thong, presumably to prevent the panels gaping, is stretched from rings attached just above the inner corners of cut-outs on the outer corner of each of the defences. All edges are bound with rawhide, creating a raised border.

Variations of shoulder reinforcements on these

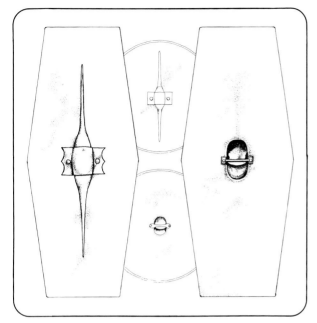

Front and rear faces of a Celtic hexagonal 'infantry' and a round 'cavalry' shield. Both would be of oak construction, covered with hide or felt, and decorated with painted designs on the front. Most fittings were of iron. The large 'infantry' body shield was normally hexagonal, rectangular or oval; the smaller 'cavalry' type, round or oval.

in sculpted examples. Bosses were of iron and included the simple wide strap types, 'butterfly' plates and conventional round varieties on circular mounting plates. It is almost certain that most shields, decorated with animal, geometric or symbolic emblems, were painted carefully in polychromatic schemes.

'Parade' shields

Oblong 'parade' shields of thin bronze sheet backed with wood have been found in the Thames at Battersea and in the Witham in Lincolnshire; they are exceptional in that applied embossed metal adorns the shield faces, and it seems clear that they were not intended for use in battle.

Swords

Celtic warriors were primarily thought of as swordsmen in the ancient world. They were employed as shock troops in Greece, Western Asia, Egypt and in the armies of Carthage.

Early Celtic iron swords were of excellent quality and followed the style of late Bronze Age types. Both bronze and iron types were manufactured together, until in time bronze ceased to be used. The stronger iron weapons were seemingly confined to the 'royal' group of warriors living in an area of central Europe around Bavaria, Wurttenberg, Baden, Alsace-Lorraine, Burgundy and the Auvergne.

Badly damaged statue from the great Gallic *oppidum* of Entremont, showing a warrior squatting in Celtic fashion. Dating from the 2nd century BC, this piece does show quite clearly the mail corselet with a cape-like shoulder reinforcement and some kind of fastening on the chest. The detail view shows, indistinctly, the remains of the sword, and the lower edge of the mail. (Musée Granet, Aix-en-Provence)

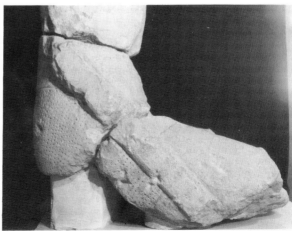

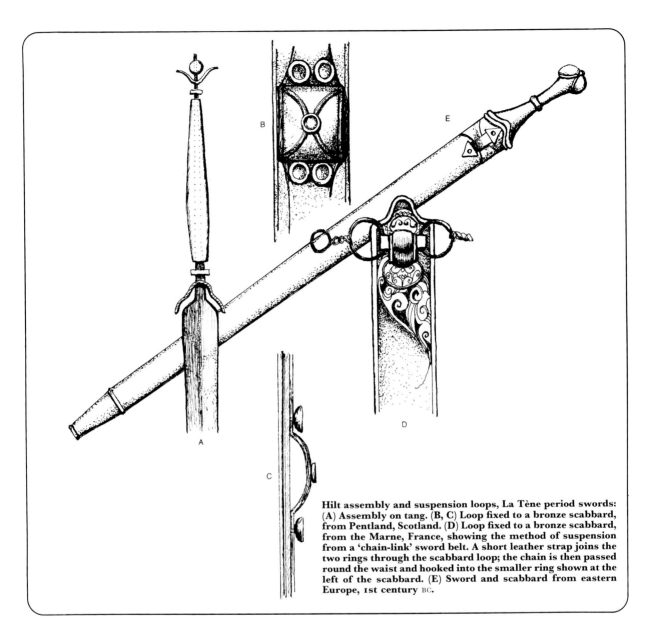

Hilt assembly and suspension loops, La Tène period swords: (A) Assembly on tang. (B, C) Loop fixed to a bronze scabbard, from Pentland, Scotland. (D) Loop fixed to a bronze scabbard, from the Marne, France, showing the method of suspension from a 'chain-link' sword belt. A short leather strap joins the two rings through the scabbard loop; the chain is then passed round the waist and hooked into the smaller ring shown at the left of the scabbard. (E) Sword and scabbard from eastern Europe, 1st century BC.

Several of the iron swords of this (Halstatt) period are so large that some experts have thought them to be for ceremonial use only, but they are no bigger than some of the great war swords of the Middle Ages. As with the bronze swords of this period, the blade is of a graceful elongated leaf shape with rounded spatular, square-kink or shallow 'V' points. Late Halstatt swords included a type with a short, thick blade and an acute point. The hilts of both types of Halstatt iron swords are distinctive. Most earlier large swords have hilts similar to bronze prototypes but are of 'Mexican hat' profile; the smaller, late Halstatt swords, also adapted from earlier bronze examples, have two prongs divided at the top of the hilt to form horns or 'antennae'. Other hilts were of a design based on the human figure and are known as 'anthropoid'— some daggers of the period also follow this fashion.

The swords of the Celtic Iron Age La Tène culture range in size from about 55 cm to 80 cm, hilt guard to point, but some reach a blade length of 90 cm. The quality of metal used in these weapons warrants the description of steel rather than iron. Quality varies, but few surviving blades descend to the poor quality described by Polybius, the Greek historian, who says of them that: '. . . they are effective only at the first blow; thereafter they are blunt, and bend so that if the warrior has no time to

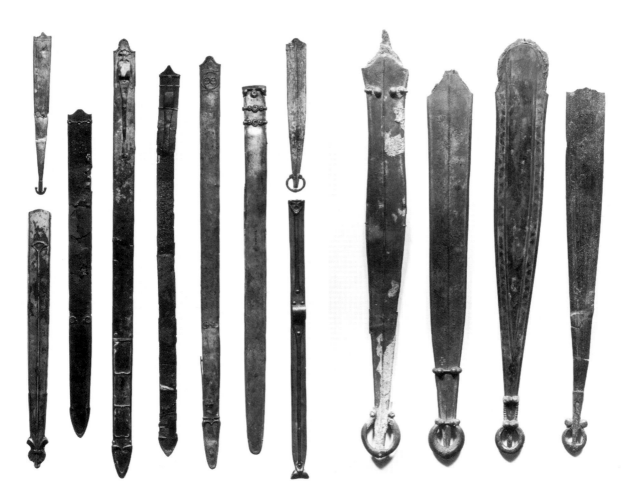

La Tène sword and dagger scabbards from Britain and Continental Europe. (British Museum)

Short bronze sword scabbards of the La Tène period found in Britain. (British Museum)

wedge it against the ground and straighten it with his foot, the second blow is quite ineffective.'

The lake at La Tène was a Celtic sacrificial site in which hundreds of swords have been found. Other sites, in France, Britain, Spain, Switzerland, Denmark, southern Germany and eastern Europe have all produced various examples of La Tène swords.

Most swords of the early La Tène period measure about 65 cm to 75 cm overall and are cut-and-stab weapons; the blades are pointed and the scabbard chapes are heavily patterned. They date from the mid-5th to the mid-3rd century BC. Swords of the middle La Tène period, to the late 2nd century BC, became longer and round-ended, overall length being about 85 cm to 90 cm. From the 1st century BC sword length increased to a mean overall average of 90 cm, a few examples having blades of 90 cm

without the handle. Scabbard chapes are neater and conform more to the sword's outline. La Tène swords of an insular style continued to be made in Britain after the Roman conquest of Gaul up to the end of the 1st century AD. The sword was usually suspended on the right hip from a sword belt of leather or a chain of linked iron rings; the sword was attached to the belt by means of a metal loop at the back face of the scabbard.

The gradual change of the La Tène sword from a fairly short cut-and-thrust weapon to a longer weapon solely designed for cutting seems to have been reversed in Britain, where points reappear on surviving blades during the last two centuries before the Roman conquest.

Spears
Spears and javelins of bronze and iron took various

71

forms and sizes. In general, spearheads were larger during the first and second La Tène phases, from the 5th to the first quarter of the 1st century BC. The most typical Celtic designs have edges curving inwards from the belly of the blade to its tip, giving the impression of an elongated point. Two spears complete with shafts were found at La Tène, and were just under 2.5 m long; butt spikes were of socketed or tanged fitting.

Bows were evidently used in some areas by some warriors. The sling—the simplest and cheapest of all missile weapons, but one demanding long practice for accuracy—was also used. The great dumps of sling 'ammunition' found on some Celtic defended sites have already been mentioned. The effectiveness of the sling-stone should never be underestimated. Large 'cobblestones' hurled at great speed could inflict fatal crushing injuries even upon soldiers protected by metal helmets, and

many hits must have produced major limb fractures. There is a school of thought which holds that the very design of the ramparts round Celtic hill forts was dictated by the widespread introduction of the sling, to produce the most effective 'fields of fire' and 'killing zones'.

The Celtic chariot

'I see a chariot of fine wood with wickerwork, moving on wheels of white bronze. A pole of white silver with a mounting of white bronze. Its frame very high, of creaking copper, rounded and firm. A strong carved yoke of gold; two firm-plaited yellow reins; the shafts hard and straight as sword-blades.' This description from *The Wooing of Emer*, an Irish legend of the Ulster Cycle, should not be taken as a literal specification; and of course, it long post-dates the period of Roman-Celtic confrontation. But experience proves that such oral traditions are extraordinarily long-lived; and leading experts such as Dr Anne Ross do believe that the Irish legends are precious survivals of the earliest Celtic culture which we can glimpse.

'Anthropoid' swords and hilts: **(A) Bronze, from N. Grimston, Yorkshire. (B) Bronze, from Chatillon-sur-Indra, France. (C) Bronze hilt, iron blade, from the River Witham, Lincolnshire. (D) Bronze hilt, iron blade, from Mainz, Germany. All** *c.* **1st century** BC.

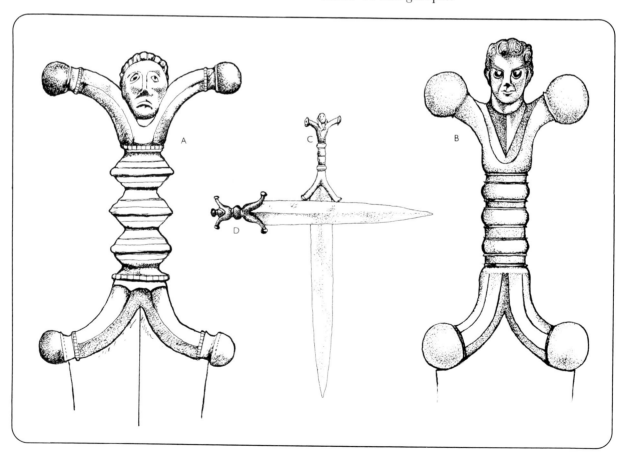

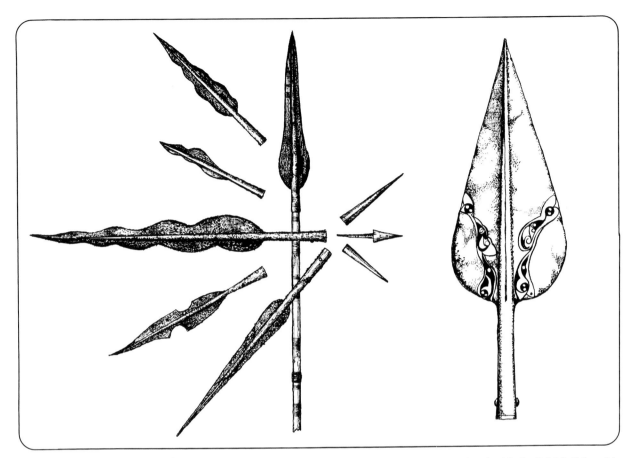

Celtic spear and javelin heads, and three butt-spikes, from La Tène, the Marne district, Alesia, and southern England. (Right) An iron spearhead inlaid with bronze patterns in the 'insular La Tène' style associated with the British Celts; this superb weapon was found in the River Thames at Datchet, Berkshire, and dates from the 1st century BC.

In about 1580 BC the Hyksos peoples, after some 200 years of occupation, were expelled from Egypt. Soon afterwards, the well-trained chariot squadrons which were the Hyksos' legacy to Egypt were spearheading invasions of the 'fertile crescent' as far north as Syria. Both the Indo-European Hyksos charioteers and their Egyptian pupils used a light, flexible two-wheeled car pulled by spirited horses. In the 1st century AD, Indo-European Celts were using the last examples of these chariots against the legions of Rome.

The Celtic battle chariot was a two-wheeled vehicle with an oblong platform secured above the axle at the centre of its length. On each side of the platform side panels were formed by double semi-circular bows of wood filled in with inserts of wood, leather, wickerwork, or a combination of these materials. According to recent authoritative opinion, the trace reins were attached to the axle housing by metal lugs in order to transfer the pull directly to the wheels. The centre pole was connected to the axle housing and the platform. (The Celts' chariot tactics are mentioned below, immediately before the section on Alesia.)

Cavalry

Gallic nobles and their immediate following filled the ranks of the cavalry. We may suppose that most wore metal helmets, and the nobles and richer retainers the mail corselets described above. Besides swords they would have carried spears and javelins. Gallic cavalry shields seem generally to have been round or oval, but some were of truncated oval shape—i.e. ovals with the top and bottom cut off square. Cavalry tactics were normally simple: a shower of javelins were thrown, and followed up by a charge using spears and swords. Gallic cavalry— the 'knights' mentioned by Caesar—were the later equivalent of the noble charioteers of an earlier period. They were apparently well mounted, on horses measuring about 14 hands (1.42 m from the ground to the withers).

Celtic saddles were constructed with a pommel on each corner of the seat unit, as shown by sculptural evidence. A later Roman saddle of the same pattern, reconstructed from the sculptural evidence and surviving fragments, is neatly seamed and stitched, with bronze stiffeners inserted into the pommels, and patterns of bronze studs on the oblong side panels. Metal discs and other ornaments were attached to the harness. Both bar and jointed snaffle bits were used, the latter apparently being more popular.

It is logical to 'work backwards from the Romans' in any reconstruction of Celtic cavalry. As early as the Gallic Wars Rome was hiring formed units of mercenary cavalry among the pacified Gallic tribes, and Gaul (together with Thrace) continued to supply the Roman army with the bulk of its auxiliary cavalry force for centuries. Clearly Celtic features remain identifiable in cavalry accoutrements long after the incorporation of the Celtic lands into the Empire.

Warfare

The Gaul, whether on foot or mounted, was primarily a swordsman.

The mass of infantry warriors were the most formidable part of a Gallic army; they fought as 'heavy' infantry, coming into direct contact with enemy troops. After some time spent slashing the air with their long swords, pouring abuse on the enemy, rhythmically banging their weapons on their shields and tossing their standards to the harsh braying of war trumpets, the tall swordsmen rolled forward like an incoming wave and began a screaming run towards enemy lines. At about 30

Roman marble copy of an original bronze statue forming part of a group erected at Pergamene by Attalos I. The statues commemorated Attalos's victory over the Celts of Asia Minor (the Galatae or 'Galatians') in 240 BC. This superb piece is now known as 'The Dying Gaul'; note the torc, the moustache, and the spiky effect of the hair, perhaps lime-washed? (Museo Capitolina, Rome)

Early La Tène period chieftain and warriors,
late 5th century BC

A

Gallic warriors of Middle La Tène period,
3rd-2nd century BC

B

Gallic cavalrymen of Late La Tène period,
1st century BC

C

British Belgic charioteer and nobleman, 1st century BC

D

Late Gallic warriors, c.52 BC

Celtic light infantry types,
1st century BC/1st century AD

F

**Guard cavalrymen, Roman army,
early 2nd century AD**

G

yards they began to discharge their javelins; within seconds, individual warriors were using their powerful physique to break up the opposing ranks.

If this first assault failed, a whole series of these attacks would be mounted, separated by short rest periods. The charges would last until the enemy was battered into defeat, or the Gauls became exhausted and retired, or just stood their ground in defiance.

These furious attacks were countered by Roman legions using javelin volleys, followed by an alternating-rank exchange system which put fresh or rested troops into the fighting line after a given period of action.

Polybius, born at the beginning of the 2nd century BC, would not only have gleaned the information he needed from official sources; it is entirely possible that he also took evidence from living witnesses to the events of 225 BC, when the Gauls of northern Italy marched on Rome. He names the Boii, Insubres and Taurisci of the Alpine region as the most likely participants. Adventurers from beyond the Alps were also invited to take part in the campaign; Polybius says that the Italian Gauls '. . . pointed out to them the great wealth of the Romans and the plunder that victory would bring . . .' The host was, in this way, swollen by large numbers of experienced Gaulish warriors from the Rhône Valley.

Rome was aware of her danger; the panic-stricken citizens sent the army and large numbers of reserves to the north, '. . . for the old terror of the Gauls lay in their bones.' The large defence force was joined by contingents from other Italian peoples including the Gallic Cenomani and Illyrian Veneti. Two armies now faced the Gauls, both large and powerful. A further territorial army of older men and boys stood behind them. A Greek man and woman and a Celtic couple were sacrificed by being buried alive by Roman officials to counter a prophecy that Greeks and Gauls would one day take all Roman land.

After the initial success of a clever deception, the Gauls were trapped on Cape Telamon between two Roman army groups, and went into laager behind two- and four-wheeled chariots. Amid a chaotic clamour from the Italian Gauls, the Gaesatae warriors from the north threw off their clothes and attacked the Roman lines with missiles. After a Gallic cavalry charge had failed, the infantry

Iron snaffle bit of the La Tène period from Marin-Epagnier, Switzerland. The Celts were keen horsemen, and made many items of horse furniture which were later adopted virtually unchanged by the Romans. Apart from the simple snaffle, examples of the more complex and much harsher curb bit have also been found.

furiously attacked the enemy. The naked Gaesatae, tall spearmen decked with golden bracelets and torcs and with their tawny manes stiffened with lime, repeatedly bounded up to the embattled legions behind their shields, and in 'senseless rage stormed against the enemy'.

In their utter frustration the Gauls refused to retreat, and 40,000 were said to have died. Some 10,000 were taken prisoner, including Aneroestes, one of the two kings; the other king and his companions died by their own hand.

The naked trans-Alpine Gauls were paralleled in other Celtic groups, and neither Diodorus Siculus nor Polybius understood the true significance of their stripping for battle. The name 'Gaesatae' is derived from *gae*, Celtic for spear or dart, and means spearman. They were tribeless young men who hired themselves out to any who would pay or share booty. It seems almost certain that they were also fey, legendary warriors. These warrior hirelings are echoed in Ireland where, during the early Middle Ages, the Fenian bands resembled the Gaesatae and were described in old Irish tales as 'ecland, without a tribe'.

The Cimbrian Wars

A quarter of a century after their brutal sack of Carthage and destruction of Corinth, the Romans controlled Spain, Greece, southern Gaul, north Africa, Lydia, Phrygia and the Mediterranean. Apart from internal political unrest their horizons were untroubled and secure. This relative calm was disrupted by reports of a movement south by large numbers of nomadic northern barbarians. According to the Roman writer Plutarch the warriors numbered about 300,000, not counting their families. Two tribes of unknown origin, named as the Cimbri and Teutones, were following an aimless southerly route past modern Magdeburg, Dresden and Vienna. In the area now known as Bohemia they were confronted by the Gaulish Boii, and were persuaded to move on peacefully.

South of the Danube, near modern Belgrade, they fought the Scordisci, a powerful tribe of Danubian Gauls. They were defeated, and turned west along the Drava into Noricum (Austria). By 113 BC the great horde was approaching the territory of the Taurisci, a Gallic people who had a protection treaty with Rome. With invasion imminent, they called for Roman aid. Carbo, the consul for that year, arrived with a large army, and

the Cimbri and Teutones prepared to move away. The Roman consul was not interested in peaceful retreats, however, and forced the barbarians to give battle at Norcia. His generalship did not match his lust for glory and the legions were only saved from total annihilation by a heavy thunderstorm. Carbo took poison, true to Republican tradition. Although confident in their ability to face the legions, the horde turned to the north-west away from Italy. During the next three years they lived among the foothills of the Alps, near the source of the Danube.

By 110 BC the wanderers had crossed the Rhine near Schaffhausen through to the Jura and down into Gaul, where they were joined by the Tigurini and other Gauls. The Roman consul of 109 BC, M. Julius Silanus, had been sent with an army into

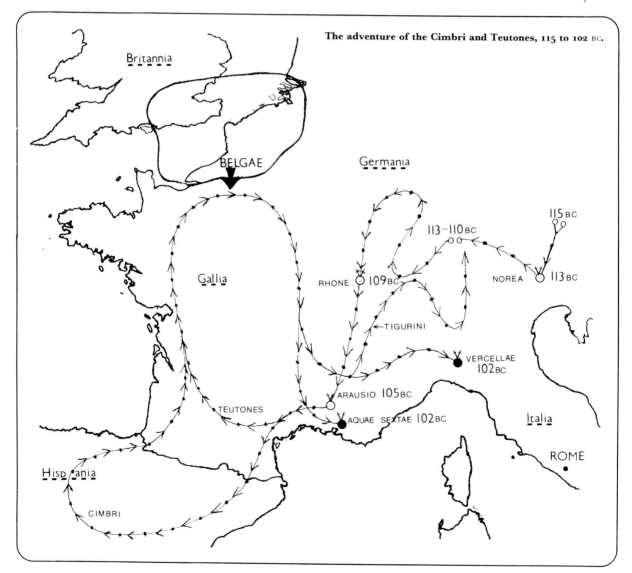

The adventure of the Cimbri and Teutones, 115 to 102 BC.

eastern Gaul, where he was met by a demand from the Cimbri and Teutones for land. The demand was rejected by Rome. The consular army went into action, and was seriously defeated in the valley of the Rhône. Other Gaulish tribes became restive as news of the second Roman disaster spread. The invaders now moved north, where they rested. Those Helvetian Gauls who had reinforced the Cimbrian horde settled along the northern frontier of Roman Gaul.

In 107 BC the Volcae-Tectosages—Gauls long established in Roman territory around modern Toulouse—rose in revolt, but were met and defeated by an army commanded by the consul L. Cassius Longinus; the army then proceeded to push the Tigurini down the valley of the Garonne. The Romans were almost destroyed and Longinus was killed when they ran into an ambush. The survivors reached the Roman camp, where their lives were bought for half the baggage and the disgrace of 'passing under the yoke' in a submission ritual.

Having received a triumph for a Spanish campaign, Q. Servilius Caepio, the consul in 106 BC, was thought to be a competent soldier. He restored calm among the Volcae. Re-conquering Toulouse, he was joined by Cn. Mallius Maximus, an ambitious provincial of consular rank, with a second army; the two commanders quarrelled, but managed to place their armies on the northern side of the Rhône under Mallius's orders when it was learned that the Cimbri and Teutones were on the move down the Rhône valley. On 6 October 105 BC, at Arausio (Orange), the Roman advance guard was wiped out. By mid-morning the consular army of Caepio was heavily engaged with the barbarian host. The Romans finally broke and the invaders swept on to assault the army of Mallius. They reached the Roman camp about an hour later. The Romans were trapped against the river, where they fought to the death. Both generals managed to escape.

In 104 BC Gaius Marius was given a second consulship by election—an emergency measure which violated a regulation of the senate. Now 25, he was a born soldier; and he completely re-structured the Roman army. The legionary ceased to be a short-service citizen levy, and became a professional heavy infantryman supported by a secondary army of auxiliaries. The new army was

Bronze helmet with a central reinforcement mounted with stud finials, dating from the 1st century BC. (Schweiz Landesmuseum, Zurich)

drilled, trained and toughened to the last degree.

Meanwhile the barbarians bypassed Italy after the victory at Arausio, and strolled through the countryside of western Gaul and northern Spain before doubling back to vanish once more into the north.

In 102 BC they materialised in the south of Provence. Marius moved quickly, racing north from Rome to join his army in fortified camp on the lower Rhône. He knew now that his army faced three pugnacious tribes confident of their ability to deal with any Roman opposition; although they had been repulsed by the Belgae in northern Gaul, their spirit was unshaken. They now made a tactical error, dividing their forces in face of the enemy: the Teutones and Ambrones followed the coast road from the west, and after attacking Roman positions without success, they broke off and made for the Italian passes. Marius (now in his fourth consulate) broke camp, and by carefully planned forced marches overtook them, arriving at Aquae Sextae (Aix-en-Provence) to await the barbarians in prepared positions across the valley. The Ambrones arrived and attacked immediately; reaching the entrenched Roman positions, they were almost completely destroyed. The next day the Teutones offered battle, and were soundly beaten by a surprise attack in the rear; most were killed or captured.

The Cimbri, who had crossed the Brenner Pass,

now faced the army of Catulus, a senatorial general, at Tridentum (Trento). His army refused to fight, and he had to abandon Italian Gaul retreating over the Po. Marius cancelled his triumph, and joined Catulus on the Po with his army. They crossed the river in high summer 101 BC, and met the Cimbri at Campi Raurii near Vercellae.

The king of the Cimbri trotted his pony out to challenge Marius to single combat for the prize of Italy. He was told that it was not the Roman custom. Plutarch writes that the Cimbrian infantry then advanced in a huge square, 30 furlongs long on each side. These warriors each had two javelins and a sword. The cavalry, about 15,000 strong, wore helmets in the form of animal heads adorned with feather plumes; they carried white shields, and wore iron breast plates. With the sun in their eyes and unused to an Italian heatwave, the Cimbrian infantry met the legions in a cloud of dust. The foremost ranks of northern warriors were chained together through their belts to present an unbroken line. Nearly all were killed. The women slaughtered some survivors, and then killed themselves. Some 60,000 prisoners were said to have been taken, and the dead numbered well over 120,000. 'Never had the scavenging birds of Italy fed on such gigantic corpses.' The Tigurini turned back to Switzerland, where they settled.

The great invasion epic was at an end. Marius had become a demi-god; but Carbo, Silanus, Mallius and Caepio were in disgrace, and five Roman armies had been destroyed. The importance of taking complete control of Gaul now became obvious, as a sure defence for the Roman heartlands south of the Alps.

Posidonius of Apamea, the leading Greek scholar of his day, journeyed to Massilia (Marseilles) and Spain from Rome during the last quarter of the 1st century BC in order to find out whether the three invading tribes were or were not Celts. His first conclusion was that nothing was known or could be known of the Cimbri; they had come out of the north to appear among the Scordisci (Celts), then passed through the Taurisci (Celts) and on to the Helvetic tribes—also Celts. Two of the three tribes of the Helvetic league were so impressed by these unspoiled tribesmen that they joined them: these were the Tigurini and Teutoni. Posidonius was able to visit the battlefield of Aquae Sextae; and as the

Conical bronze helmet found in the north of England and dating from the 2nd century BC. The large neck guard has a thick fold of metal reinforcement at the junction with the skull, and a heavy curvilinear motif at the centre. The skull rim is rolled over, and there is a curvilinear design on either side. The raised, hatched studs were originally richly enamelled. (Meyrick Coll., British Museum)

guest of the Greeks of Massilia and of Celtic nobles he enjoyed access to first-hand knowledge not shared by any scholar of his own day or since. He was able to speak to people who had seen the barbarians for themselves. Modern opinion is that the Cimbri were one of the tribes of the Germani group of northern Celts; all the known names of their leaders are pure Celtic. The Teutoni and Tigurini were, as Posidonius stated, Helvetic Celts, and the Ambrones were a tribe related to them.

The Gallic Wars
In 59 BC Gaius Julius Caesar, an ambitious and able Roman politician then aged 41, was named consul and, the following year, governor of Gallia Cisalpina (northern Italy) and Illyricum in the Roman-occupied Balkans. Just before his departure for Illyricum the governor-designate of Gallia Narbonensis (Roman-occupied southern Gaul) died, and this province was added to Caesar's responsibilities. This multiple governorship presented him with great opportunities. It lay immediately adjacent to free Gaul, in whose political affairs Rome already interfered constantly: any attempt to unify the country was frustrated by Roman agents. Northern Italy was a great recruiting-ground for troops. Caesar had established a military reputation against the Celtiberians and Lusatians in Spain in 61–60 BC; a conquest of

free Gaul would consolidate it, and offered the chance of amassing great wealth at a time when Caesar was seriously in debt.

In free Gaul one Dumnorix, a prince of the Aedui and a successful financier, assembled a considerable following. His brother Divitiacus, the tribal leader, opposed his rise, and in 60 BC fled to Rome where he became friendly with Cicero. Divitiacus claimed that Dumnorix planned to take over first the Aedui, and later the whole of Gaul: he had allied himself with the Sequani, who had agreed to allow the German Suevi to take over lands in Alsace in return for their serving as auxiliaries under Dumnorix. Towards the end of 59 BC and in early 58 the influx of German tribesmen began a pattern of migration which would offer Caesar his chance to become involved in Gallic affairs.

The Germans poured across the territory of the Helvetii, who decided to destroy their crops and villages and fall back into Gaul. At the Rhône they asked permission to cross Roman-dominated territory occupied by the Allobroges. Caesar refused them passage, and barred their way with a scratch force of available troops. The Helvetii changed direction in the Jura, descending the passes directly into free Gaul through Sequanian territory. Caesar's reports to the Senate painted the Helvetii in lurid colours as murderers, rapists and land-grabbers, thus justifying his reinforcement of his army with troops from the northern Italian garrisons. He moved swiftly forward into free Gaul, meeting the Helvetii at Bibracte (Autun) and inflicting a sound defeat and many losses. The survivors were driven back into their Swiss tribal lands.

The Roman Senate was apathetic, and Caesar was a skilled political manipulator. With the indirect support of his client Divitiacus, who pleaded for Roman confirmation of his rightful leadership of the Aedui, Caesar was able to

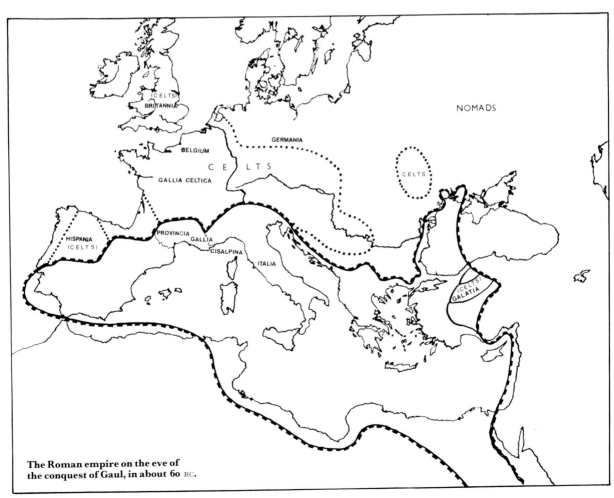

The Roman empire on the eve of the conquest of Gaul, in about 60 BC.

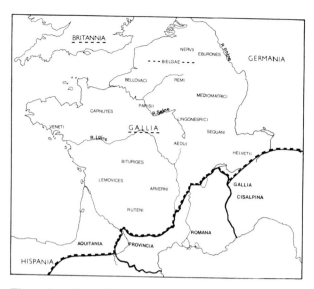

The major tribes of Gaul, in about 60 BC.

manoeuvre the Senate into accepting his rôle as 'protector of the Gauls', thus giving him an almost free hand. Many Gauls must have realised at this time that both Rome and the Germanic tribes from the east were strong enough to take control of their lands. The question of which conqueror might best serve the Gauls' interests became academic. Germanic incursions provided Caesar with all the excuse he needed to push forward into Gaul himself.

In 58 BC he defeated the Germanic Suevi, led by Ariovistus, in Alsace, and planted garrisons in Sequanian territory east of the Saône. In 57 BC the resistance of the Belgae of northern Gaul to the establishment of Roman positions on the Aisne was overcome; the chronic disunity of the Celts caused the Belgae to break up into tribal groups, which were defeated piecemeal. In the same year Caesar's lieutenant Publius Licinius Crassus subdued present-day Normandy and Brittany. On the Sambre Caesar defeated the Nervii and Atuatucres, surviving dangerous situations by his coolness in command, which allowed him to turn the fearless impetuosity of the Celts against themselves.

In 56 BC the Veneti, occupying south-west Brittany, started a revolt which was supported by the still-unconquered Morini of the Pas de Calais and the Menapii of the lower Rhine. The Veneti were notable for having a large fleet of ships at their disposal; they carried on an active trade with their Belgic cousins across the Channel in southern Britain, and levied a toll on other ships plying their

stretch of the Atlantic coast. In 56 Crassus was in winter quarters in Venetic territory with the VIIth Legion. Food ran short, and Crassus sent officers out to obtain supplies from neighbouring tribes. The tribunes sent to the Veneti, Titus Sillius and Quintus Vellanius, were promptly made prisoner; and this example was copied by the other tribes. A message was sent to Crassus, demanding his release of Gallic hostages in return for his officers' safety.

Caesar, then touring eastern Gaul and Illyricum, was informed, and at once ordered the construction of ships on the Loire and the recruitment of crews in Roman Gaul to the south. Examples of Mediterranean types of warship built included the heavy quinquereme, the medium trireme, and the light liburnium. The Venetic ships were apparently of fairly massive construction, made from heavy timbers joined with iron bolts, and powered not by oars but solely by large leather sails; they had a shallow draught, and high gunwales to protect the crews from missile weapons.

The sea battle took place at Quiberon near Lorient in the autumn of 56 BC. The Romans slashed the rigging of the Venetic ships with long-handled sickles; and the Celtic seamen's fate was sealed when the wind dropped, allowing their becalmed *pontones* to be captured one by one by the handier, oar-powered Roman ships. The Veneti were ruthlessly punished for their revolt, and the Morini and Menapii later suffered the same fate.

In 55 BC the tireless Caesar wiped out the Germanic Tencteri and Usipete, who had crossed the lower Rhine the previous winter. He bridged the Rhine near Koblenz and raided on the German bank; and in the same season he led a small expeditionary force to Britain.

The British expedition
It should be remembered that to the Celts the Channel was probably just a particularly marked geographical frontier between closely related Belgic peoples. There was constant contact across it; and Rome was already profiting by this to follow her usual method of 'softening up' potential future conquests, by interfering in tribal and dynastic quarrels. Caesar writes that before he crossed the Channel he had received envoys from some British tribes offering submission to Rome; and that they were accompanied on their return to Britain by one

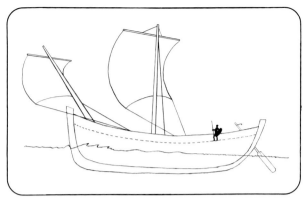

Possible reconstruction of the type of ship used by the sea-going Veneti tribe of northern Gaul in the 1st century BC.

Commius, supported by Caesar as the chief of a powerful southern British tribe, the Atrebates. Commius was ordered to urge other tribal leaders to trust Rome, and to warn them of Caesar's coming.

His expeditions into southern Britain in 55 BC, and again the following year, were certainly not planned as invasions; he lacked the resources for occupation, and the most important military reason for making the crossings was probably to discourage support for the Britons' rebellious cousins in northern Gaul. The first raid was resisted by the Cantiaci tribe of Kent; and in the relevant passage of Caesar's book on his Gallic Wars he leaves us this impression of Celtic chariot tactics:

'In chariot fighting, the Britons drive all over the field hurling javelins, and generally the terror inspired by the horses and the noise of the chariot wheels is sufficient to throw their opponents' ranks into disorder. Then, after making their way between the squadrons of their own cavalry, they [i.e. the high class warriors riding in the chariots] jump down and engage the enemy on foot. In the meantime the charioteers retire a short distance . . . and place the chariots in such a position that their masters, if hard pressed . . . have an easy means of retreat. . . . By daily training and practice they attain such proficiency that even on a steep slope they are able to control the horses at full gallop, and check and turn them in a moment. They can run along the chariot pole, stand on the yoke, and get back into the chariot as quick as lightning.'

Alesia
The disunity of the Gallic Celts had allowed Caesar

to pick off the tribes one by one, despite the fact that he enjoyed no great superiority of forces, and had even enabled him to enlist the very effective Celtic cavalry as allies in various campaigns. These years had, nevertheless, seen several determined attempts to resist Roman expansion. Dumnorix of the Aedui had been hacked down when he refused to be deported to Britain. Indutiomarus, besieging a Roman strongpoint in 54 BC, had ridden away from it when he lost patience with the delay—only to be pursued by the defenders, who brought his head back to headquarters. Ambiorix was defeated too many times by Caesar, and finally took to the forests with only four faithful riders. Other leaders were captured and executed, some by the torture which Caesar claims was 'according to the customs of their ancestors'. But the greatest challenge to Roman expansion came in 52 BC, from a widespread resistance movement led by Vercingetorix, son of Celtillus of the royal house of the Averni.

Vercingetorix was fanatically anti-Roman, and a leader of real ability; and he was willing to use any means to his end. He urged a 'scorched earth' policy, so as to avoid pitched battles and sieges while cutting the Romans off from supplies. Villages were burned to the ground, wells poisoned, roads destroyed, and the countryside stripped of crops and livestock. But not all the tribes were willing to pay this price. Vercingetorix was unable to persuade the Bituriges to destroy and abandon their chief settlement of Avaricum (Bourges); the tribal leaders threw themselves at his feet and pleaded for their town. His warning of the consequences was vindicated when Caesar took Avaricum after a difficult siege.

Caesar's troops were subjected to ambush and attack from all sides, and their supply lines and stores were constantly being destroyed. Knowing Vercingetorix to be in the vicinity, Caesar besieged Gergovia near Clermont-Ferrand, a strong position easily defended from behind ten-foot perimeter walls built on the crest of a range of hills. The garrison repulsed an attempted storming, and the Gallic army was able to launch an overwhelming attack from outside the walls on the troops occupied with the siege. By the time Caesar retired from the field that night he had lost 700 men and 36 centurions—his first outright defeat in Gaul.

A major ambush followed; but Vercingetorix was

Bronze armlets from Scotland, 2nd/1st century BC; the finials have coloured paste inserts.

unable to control his hot-headed followers, and what had been intended as a feint attack to separate a Roman column led by Caesar from its baggage train turned into a fatal reality. In their battle-madness the Celts charged anything in their path, and were methodically slaughtered in the customary manner by the superbly disciplined legions. Vercingetorix retired with his own forces to Alesia on the Seine (modern Alise-Ste. Reine). He was followed by Caesar with about 3,000 infantry and a force of mercenary Germanic cavalry. On arrival before the walls, Caesar decided to adopt the classic method of circumvallation, and built his own surrounding wall all round the site. While the legionaries built their wall the Gauls harried them with hit-and-run sorties, and sent riders out to summon aid from other tribes. Vercingetorix stayed inside Alesia, the centre and figurehead of Gallic resistance.

Caesar made use of every resource of Roman military skill in preparing the containing defences. A complicated series of dry ditches were dug; a tributary of the Seine was diverted to fill a moat; and large areas were sewn with caltrops and 'lillies'—sharp stakes sunk in pits. Walls were built facing both inwards towards Alesia, and outwards towards any would-be relieving army of Gauls; the

outer rampart was all of 15 miles long. Caesar's besiegers thus occupied a ring around the town, defended front and rear.

After a month's siege the defenders of Alesia expelled the women, children, old and sick from the *oppidum* to save useless mouths. They were not allowed to leave the site by the Romans, and presumably they gradually perished in the no-man's-land between the armies. Soon afterwards a Gallic relief army arrived outside the Roman lines; Caesar puts their numbers at 250,000 infantry and 8,000 horsemen, drawn from 41 tribes. Like all figures quoted by ancient and medieval historians, these are probably wildly exaggerated; even so, the threatening host must have been considerable. Caesar was now sandwiched between two hostile armies, and his forces were soon subjected to furious attacks from both inside and outside.

Towards evening on the first day of this battle Caesar used his Germanic cavalry to throw the Gauls back from the outer ring of walls; the advantage was exploited by other auxiliary cavalry, the Gauls were driven back towards their camps, and missile-armed warriors supporting them were massacred.

After a day of preparation the relieving army again moved up to the assault, and simultaneously Vercingetorix sortied to attack the inner face of the Roman ring. After long and fierce fighting both attacks were driven off, losing heavily to showers of missiles which swept the 'killing zones' of caltrops and 'lillies'.

A third assault developed when desultory attacks on both inner and outer faces of Caesar's defences led to a battle for control of an awkward sector of the outward-facing lines on a piece of rising ground up the side of a plateau. During a furious attack on this sector Caesar sent in six cohorts as reinforcements, but had to follow them with another eleven cohorts stripped from the nearest neighbouring sectors along the walls. Caesar himself finally took the Gallic attackers in the rear with another four cohorts and part of the Roman cavalry; the Gauls broke off their attempt on the wall, and those who were not cut down were taken prisoner, including the leader of the assault, one Vercassivelaunus.

Disheartened, the Gallic relief army began to melt away, and Roman cavalry followed them to inflict further casualties. Caesar writes that on the following day Vercingetorix and his tribal chiefs were delivered up to the Romans, and the garrison's weapons handed over, while the general sat before his inner fortifications.

The Greek historian Plutarch, born almost a century later, gives a more Celtic flavour to the surrender. He says that Vercingetorix put on his most beautiful armour, had his horse carefully groomed, and rode out through the gates of Alesia to where Caesar was sitting; Vercingetorix rode round him in a circle, then leapt down from his horse, stripped off his armour, and sat silent and motionless at Caesar's feet until he was taken away.

He was kept in chains, reserved for Caesar's eventual triumphal procession, for six long years. In 46 BC his shrunken frame was dressed once more in his best armour; and after being paraded in Caesar's triumph Vercingetorix, son of Celtillus of the Averni, a prince of Gaul, was ritually strangled.

Over the next two years Gaul was brought under Caesar's control so completely that there were to be no further national risings even during the Roman civil wars of 49–31 BC. The utmost ruthlessness was shown towards any sign of resistance. The new province's tax yield amounted to four million sesterces; a Gallic legion was raised, and some Gallic leaders were placed on Caesar's staff. Many Gauls fled to Germany, Switzerland, eastern Europe and Britain. During the closing years of the 1st century BC the Celtic tribes in the foothills of the Alps and on the Danube were also brought into the Roman orbit.

Britain

Nearly 90 years after the assassination of Julius Caesar, Tiberius Claudius Drusus—the Emperor Claudius of Rome and her empire—succeeded his mad nephew Caligula unexpectedly, and at the sword-points of the mutinous Praetorian Guard. Shy, handicapped, and stammering, the new emperor was advised that an exploit to provide a pretext for the award of triumphal honours would be in order. The conquest of Britain offered an opportunity to accept such honours without undue risk.

In AD 43 a convenient appeal for Roman help

The major tribes of mainland Britain, in about AD 44.

against the powerful Catuvellauni tribe was received from Verica, king of the Atrebates of southern Hampshire. Claudius assembled four legions and strong auxiliary forces in Gaul, under command of Aulus Plautius. This army was shipped across the Channel, landing at Richborough and other points on the Kent coast, and establishing their supply base with, apparently, no significant interference from the Celts. Moving inland, they made a contested crossing of the River Medway, and the Celts fell back before them to the Thames. This, too, was crossed against spirited opposition; as at the Medway, the Romans committed specialist Batavian troops first, who swam their horses across under fire and established a bridgehead. On the northern bank the Romans built a fort, and awaited the arrival of the emperor.

Claudius arrived in August, bringing with him a detachment of the Praetorian Guard, and probably reinforcements in the form of vexillations from the Rhine legions (and, according to Dio Cassius, elephants!). The army which now advanced on the Catuvellaunian capital of Camulodunum (Colchester) was built around the four original legions of the invasion force: the IInd Augusta from Strasbourg, the XIVth Gemina from Mainz, the XXth Valeria from Neuss, and the IXth Hispana from Hungary. All these units were experienced in fighting northern European warriors. The auxiliary force—which probably equalled the legionary infantry in number—included the Batavians from modern Holland, and many other cohorts of Germans, Gauls and Thracians. Camulodunum was captured without difficulty. Here Claudius received the formal submission of a number of tribes; and then returned to Rome, after a stay of only two weeks, and well before the onset of the miserable northern winter. Rome celebrated his triumph, and the army left in Britain set about crushing the inland Celtic tribes.

The XXth Legion remained at Colchester; the IInd, commanded by the future emperor Vespasian, headed a column which moved across the West Country to subdue the Atrebates, Dobunni and Durotriges; the XIVth were sent into the West Midlands to deal with the Cornovii; and the IXth headed north towards the lands of the Coritani. By AD 47 this army had given Rome a British province up to a line running from the Bristol Channel in the

south-west to the Humber in the north-east. The only individual operations of which we have any mention are those of the IInd Augusta; according to Suetonius they fought 30 battles, conquered two tribes (almost certainly the Dobunni and Durotriges), and captured 20 towns and the Isle of Wight. Excavations at Maiden Castle and Hod Hill forts in Dorset have unearthed dramatic evidence of their storming under cover of barrages of catapult bolts.

Between AD 47 and 60 the Roman forces were intermittently but heavily engaged in Wales, against the Silures of the south-east and the Ordovices of the central highlands—the latter apparently led by Caractacus, a son of the Catuvellaunian king, Cunobelinus.

In AD 59–60 Suetonius Paulinus, the Roman military governor of Britain, led two legions into north-west Wales. The climax of the campaign was an attack on the island of Mona (Anglesey), a druidic cult centre which was fiercely defended. He swam his cavalry across the Menai Strait, accompanied by the infantry in flat-bottomed boats. In bloody fighting embittered by the evidence of hideous atrocities and by the presence of shrieking druids whipping up the Celtic warriors, the sanctuary was wiped out. While the army paused in Wales, ready to crush any remaining resistance, there came news of a disaster to the east.

Boudicca

The Iceni were a Belgic tribe occupying areas in Suffolk, Norfolk and Cambridgeshire. At the time of the invasion their king Antedios diplomatically allied the tribe to Rome, thus avoiding conquest and slavery for his people, and preserving his personal wealth. When the XXth Legion left the area in AD 49 prior to the Welsh campaign, the tribe was disarmed as a precaution; this caused resentment. Antedios was soon succeeded by Prasutagus, who renewed the treaty with Rome. When he, too, died in AD 60, the Romans decided to annexe the kingdom outright. Men acting for the military governor's civil and financial counterpart, the procurator, plundered the tribal territory, causing widespread hardship and outrage. Even the king's widow, Boudicca, was flogged, and her daughters raped. The exact sequence of events is unknown; but soon afterwards the whole region

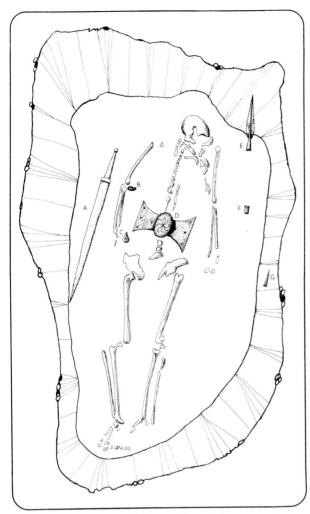

Plan of the grave of a Celtic warrior of the 1st century BC **excavated at Owlesbury, Hampshire in 1973: (A) Iron sword. (B) Bronze rings from the sword belt. (C) Silver belt hook. (D) Large bronze shield boss. (E) Iron spearhead. (F) Iron ferrule. (G) Iron butt spike.**

time-expired Roman veterans and their families. Although built within what had been the wall of a legionary fort, its defences had been neglected. The last defenders took refuge in the partly-built temple of Claudius, probably the most substantial building available; it was burnt down, and the defenders massacred. A relief force of about 2,000 men of the 1st Cohort, IXth Legion and some 500 auxiliary troopers, hurrying over open country under command of the IXth's legate, Petilius Cerialis, was wiped out somewhere north-east of Colchester, and only Cerialis and some of his cavalry escaped to Lincoln.

Verulamium (St Albans) and London were overwhelmed, and put to sack. The procurator and many of the richer citizens escaped to Gaul—some, almost certainly, by way of Bosham, on the estates of the Romanised king of the Regnenses, Cogidubnus. Those who could not escape— by far the majority—were massacred, many suffering atrocious torture.

Forced marches eventually brought Suetonius Paulinus back from his Welsh campaign, to somewhere just east of where the little River Anker is crossed by Watling Street, near Lichfield. His available troops seem to have consisted of the XIVth Legion, parts of the IInd and IXth, and about 4,500 auxiliaries.

Boudicca's Britons arrived on the field in huge numbers, the warriors in an uncontrollable mass, their families camping in a huge arc of waggons behind them. After the usual display of clashing arms, trumpeting, waving swords and deep-throated bellowing, the Celts charged the waiting cohorts. They were met in the text-book manner by two volleys of javelins followed by a legionary counter-charge. The tribesmen were pushed backwards, into and beyond a narrow defile. The lay of the ground, and the packed mass of non-combatants and waggons behind their position, combined to trap the Celts in a way which allowed the legions and the auxiliary cavalry to cut them to pieces. The fighting lasted for many hours, and the slaughter was great. This action won for the XIVth Gemina the honoured title 'Martia Victrix'. Her rebellion in ruins, Boudicca, the great red lady of the Iceni, soon died herself—there are conflicting claims for natural causes and poison.

Vexillations from the Rhine legions were shipped

boiled over into rebellion, with previously pacified tribes such as the Trinovantes joining the Iceni under Boudicca's leadership.

Writing a century after her death, the historian Dio Cassius says that Boudicca 'was tall, terrible to look on, and gifted with a powerful voice. A flood of bright red hair ran down to her knees; she wore a golden necklet made up of ornate pieces; a multi-coloured robe; and over it, a thick cloak held together by a brooch. She took up a long spear to cause dread in all who set eyes on her.'

The combined host of rebel warriors swept south. Colchester, former capital of Cunobelinus and the site of the Britons' formal surrender to the emperor, was now a Romanised town occupied largely by

to Britain to reinforce the weakened garrison. The army was kept in the field, in its leather tents, despite the onset of winter. A merciless punitive campaign laid waste the tribal territories. Finally, in AD 61, a new governor was sent out; Petronius Turpilianus replaced the terror campaign of Suetonius Paulinus with a more flexible and diplomatic policy, and conquered Britain began to be eased from tribal anarchy towards capitalist oligarchy.

Agricola

Even so, it was to be more than 20 years before Roman arms pushed the frontier of the province into the far north. It was AD 84 when Julius Agricola (a most able military governor, whose tenure had been extended to allow him to pursue a series of campaigns of northward expansion) finally stood face to face with Britain's last Celtic army. Under the leadership of Calgacus, some 30,000 Cale-

donian warriors stood at bay somewhere near Inverurie in Scotland—the exact site of 'Mons Graupius' is unknown. The Caledonians stood with their 'huge swords and short shields', dodging or artfully tipping the missiles loosed by the artillery-men. The Celtic chariots performed the usual feats of virtuosity between the two armies.

Agricola sent his Gallic and German auxiliaries in to open the attack. These semi-civilised mercenaries attacked with such élan that they had soon carved their way deep into the Celtic ranks, and were in danger of being enveloped. Roman cavalry sent forward to support them charged successfully into the enemy ranks, but could not penetrate to those gathered on a hillside behind them; the horses slipped and clambered to a halt, and some of the troopers were thrown.

Encouraged, the Caledonians charged forward to exploit their advantage—and in abandoning the high ground, gave Agricola his chance. His reserve

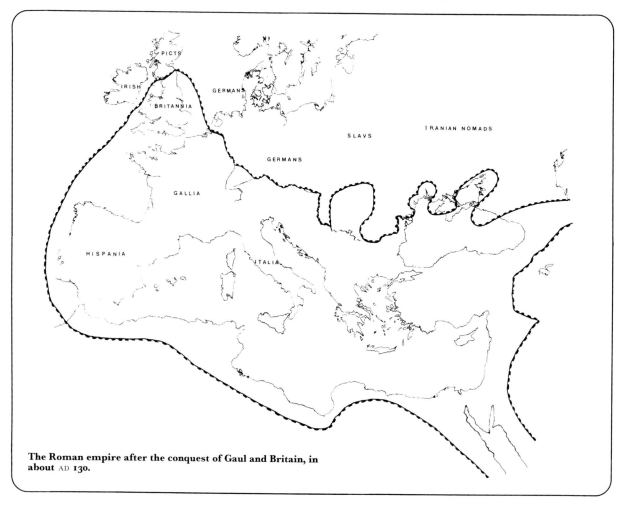

The Roman empire after the conquest of Gaul and Britain, in about AD **130.**

cavalry took them in the flank, and they broke; some fought savagely to the end, but many escaped into the hills. The legionary infantry had not been committed at all.

Archaeology suggests that at one time Rome intended to occupy at least part of the Scottish Highlands; whatever the reason, the forts were abandoned uncompleted, and the consolidation of the pacified province took place behind the barrier of Hadrian's Wall, that extraordinary feat of engineering which lies across the country from sea to sea just south of the modern English-Scottish border. Rome briefly occupied the more northerly Antonine Wall between the Firths of Clyde and Forth during the 2nd century AD; and later emperors made forays into Caledonia in response to pressure on the northern frontier. But in general, the highland fastness of Scotland remained the last free refuge of the Celtic people of Britain.

The Plates

A: Early La Tène period warriors, late 5th century BC
The chieftain A1 wears a conical bronze helmet with a peak on the front rim; the wide edging band is decorated with repoussé work in La Tène style. The breastplate, of a type used extensively in Italy, is a bronze roundel secured by crossed straps, and reinforced and decorated with repoussé studs.

The warrior A2 wears a helmet of the type discovered at Negau in Yugoslavia. This one has no crest, though most recovered examples have fore-and-aft or transverse crest fittings attached. The rims contain a template with spaced holes to accept the stitches of a lining, keeping the headpiece rim at ear level, well up on the skull. In contrast, A3 is an ordinary free tribal warrior; his only defence is a shield, and his sword is of indifferent quality. He is making a prudent offering of a gold brooch to a water sprite before setting out for war.

All three wear woollen garments, some of them in checkered pattern; A1 also has an undyed cloak of creamy new twist, and A2 wears a sleeved tunic under a thicker, sleeveless jerkin of woollen mix.

The earliest writers describe Celtic patterns as 'checkered', 'speckled', 'striped', or 'multi-coloured'. Many authorities now believe that broad, simple, symmetrical patterns are less likely for the earliest periods than quite involved, 'stripey' patterns of 'non-repeating' weaves, and we have tried here to devise suitable reconstructions. The fragmentary cloth survivals are uniformly of fine quality, woven in small, intricate patterns, though colours have naturally not survived.

The weapons carried by these warriors are of the types associated with the chariot graves of the period. The swords are mostly pointed, and measure between about 55 cm and 70 cm from point to shoulder. Some are of the highest quality, strong and flexible, with pattern-welded blades and hilts of horn, bone or wood. The chieftain A1 has a matched set of sword and dagger. Scabbards were mostly of wood covered with leather; part of one found in Scotland has a thin hazel lath pushed between the layers of one hide. Some were of iron or bronze; and large decorative chapes are typical of the early La Tène period. Examples of bronze scabbards sometimes have a 'pounced' surface, presumably imitating leather. Celtic spears are of various shapes and sizes; the small javelins have heads about 10 cm long, while some spearheads reach 50 cm long.

B: Gallic warriors of the Middle La Tène period, 3rd–2nd century BC
This was the period of the great invasions down the Italian peninsula, when the Gaesatae—a distinct group of free-wandering warriors from the Gaulish hinterland beyond the Alps—were invited south. They fought naked at the battle of Telamon; one of them is shown here as B1, but wearing a fine bronze 'Montefortino' helmet, with massive cheek guards secured by thongs through rings underneath the rear neck guard, and a horsehair crest. The torc is electrum, and the plated belt and bracelet are bronze. His weapons are a large thrusting-spear, two javelins and a sword. The latter hangs from an extra loop on the belt, engaging with a metal loop on the back surface of the scabbard. The shield is painted with curvilinear patterns.

From the Marne district, warrior B2 has a simple iron 'reversed jockey cap' helmet without cheek guards, held in place by straps from holes drilled at the lower edges of the skull; there may have been a third attachment point below the neck guard, where carrying rings were located. A bronze torc might have highly decorated finials. His short, thick woollen smock is held by a braided woollen belt, and similar strips hold the loose trousers at the ankle. The large shield has a decorative motif of linked torcs. The fairly long sword is of good quality, and he carries a dagger.

The horseman B3 is of the 2nd century. In his *Fall of the Roman Republic* Plutarch describes Cimbrian cavalry at Vercellae as wearing helmets like the gape-jawed heads of terrible beasts heightened with tall feather plumes; as carrying white shields, two javelins, and a large, heavy sword; and as wearing iron breastplates. In this possible reconstruction we draw upon known examples of Celtic war-gear of the period. The iron helmet is reconstructed after one from Ciumesti Maramures in Romania; it is mounted with a bronze bird, whose hinged wings would flap when the warrior was in violent motion. (Helmets mounted with animal images do appear on the Gundestrup cauldron, but no known Celtic helmets exactly fit Plutarch's description.) The Romanian helmet was found with a coat of bronze mail and bronze greaves; the 'iron breastplates' mentioned by Plutarch are more likely to have been iron mail corselets, as here.

C: Gallic cavalrymen of the Late La Tène period, 1st century BC

Rider C1 wears a peaked helmet from a burial in eastern Europe; it was found with the sword, a quiver, and the horse harness. His torc is gold. The short smock-tunic is finished with a pronounced fringe; and the baggy yellow and green checkered trousers are tucked into ankle boots. The standard is based on a stylised bronze casting of a boar found at Neuvy-en-Sullius, Loiret, France.

Many Celtic horsemen fought without helmets or body armour; and it seems most likely that during their life-or-death struggle with Rome some of the poorer warriors must have acquired items of captured Roman equipment which escaped ritual destruction. We show C2 wearing a captured Roman infantry helmet of a style then nearing the end of its active use, of the so-called 'Etrusco-Corinthian' type. This peculiar and degenerate development of a closed Greek Corinthian style has the eye openings and nose guard of the original facial area faintly defined on what has now become

the visor. The crest is horsehair. In the background a rider carries the great Celtic war trumpet known as a carnyx.

These riders would normally throw their javelins immediately before contact; the heavier thrusting spear would be used at close quarters, and finally the sword might be drawn. The limited monumental evidence shows cavalry shields as being of round, oval or truncated oval shape with a central spine; in other respects they would be constructed in the same way as the infantry shields known from archaeological finds, but probably had a different carrying system. Classical carvings of cavalry shields show that they could be fitted with an arm strap as well as a hand grip; the latter was attached either behind the boss or the centre of the outer spine, or between the centre and the 'leading edge' of the shield.

D: British chariot and crew, c.55 BC

The charioteer is an ordinary warrior whose body is painted with designs in woad—extract of *Isalis Tinctalia*; we show the insular La Tène decorative patterns known from British artefacts, but a simpler series of shapes could well have been used. His passenger is a Belgic nobleman, fully armed with a set of javelins, sword, and 'infantry' shield.

The chariot box is about a metre wide, mounted on wheels about 90 cm in diameter. Though not of as light construction as earlier Egyptian and Syrian examples, which were reputed to be so light that one man could carry them, the Celtic chariot was by all accounts an extremely fast and manoeuvrable vehicle; the Celts delighted in performing stunning tricks of daring and skill at high speed. The warrior was able to fight against horsemen from the chariot platform, but would dismount to fight on foot against infantry. The charioteer would stand off, ready to swoop in and pick up his nobleman in an emergency.

The chariot is shown painted, although no direct evidence exists for the practice—e.g. traces of paint on chariot parts recovered at archaeological sites, or reference to coloured finishes on the Celtic chariots mentioned in classical literature. There is reference, however, to a variety of metals being used in chariot furniture; and the old Irish epics, which some historians believe to be valid indirect evidence, describe the hero Cuchulain's red and white chariot. Finally, we can call in support of our guesswork the known Celtic love of colour and display.

E: Late Gallic warriors, c.52 BC

The horseman E1 has a crested example of the 'Agen' type of helmet as found on the site of the battle of Alesia; he has hung the helmet on one horn of his saddle, his shield on another. He wears a striped woollen jerkin over a checker-pattern long-sleeved smock, and his cloak is tied behind his saddle.

The iron helmet worn by the nobleman E2 is of the 'Port' type dating from the last phase of La Tène culture. Over a long-sleeved smock with braiding at hem and cuffs he wears a mail corselet, slit at the hips to make for an easy mounted seat.

Both these warriors could be typical of the better equipped followers of Vercingetorix during his epic rebellion. The harness fittings are based on examples from several Celtic sites of the 1st century, and the spears on types found at Alesia. The morale of these warriors will not be improved by their spotting a bloodstained rag by a stream—a Celtic omen of appalling significance.

F: Celtic light infantry types, 1st century BC/*1st century* AD

The slinger F1 represents the defenders of hill forts among the western British tribes, such as Maiden Castle, Dorset and Danebury, Hertfordshire. His stone-bag would be full of 'pebbles'—actually, cobble-sized and water-smoothed stones of uniform weight, gathered from beaches and rivers.

The bowman F2 represents the small body of archers which Vercingetorix gathered at Alesia from all over Gaul; this man is from the south-west. At the battle of Mons Graupius in AD 83,

somewhere in the Grampian Hills of Perthshire, Caledonian warriors like F3 are said to have shown skill and courage in knocking aside Roman missiles with their long swords and small shields—though they were eventually routed by Agricola's Germanic auxiliaries using Rome's classic hand-to-hand tactics.

Young men like F4, not yet strong enough to trade sword blows in the ranks of the 'assault infantry', could still give vent to their aggressive spirit as javelineers, using skills learned in their foster-fathers' homes.

G: Guard cavalrymen, Roman army, early 2nd century AD

Among the carvings from the triumphal relief in the Emperor Trajan's forum are scenes showing Trajan with members of guard units of his army. Beside the infantry stand dismounted cavalry troopers, offering their emperor the severed heads of Geto-Dacian notables. Since the days of Julius Caesar, 150 years before, large numbers of Gauls, and particularly cavalry, had been enlisted into the Roman army. At least one authority believes that some scenes in the carved relief indicate an intention in the reign of Trajan to associate auxiliary troops more closely with the mystique of the Imperial army, and that units may have been honoured with some kind of guard status. It is a fair presumption that these troopers, holding up severed heads in time-honoured Celtic fashion, may have been Gallic.

The helmets shown here, of ceremonial Attic type, may have been replaced in battle by more substantial headgear. The colours shown on these costumes are, frankly, guesswork: there is no firm evidence for guard uniform and shield colours, but a distinctive scheme seems feasible.

The Peoples of Protohistoric Spain

'By the name of Iberia, the ancient Greeks designated all the country that extends beyond the River Rhône and the isthmus which comprises the Gaulish gulf; while we today place the borders in the Pyrenees, and say that the names "Iberia" and "Hispania" are synonymous. According to others, "Iberia" does not apply to any region beyond the vicinity of the River Iberus, whose inhabitants were called Igletes. Asclepiades of Mirlea said that this was a small region. The Romans used the terms "Iberia" and "Hispania" indifferently, for the whole country, calling its internal divisions "Ulterior" and "Citerior", and being prepared to modify these terms if there arose a need for a new administrative division.' (Strabo, *Geography*, III, 4, 19.)

During the 3rd century BC, on the eve of the Second Punic War[1], we may categorise the Hispanic peoples in three major cultural and ethnic groups, as a result of long-standing mutual interaction and external influence during the First Iron Age. The group living in the north of Spain was formed by peoples having Indo-European roots, and largely 'Celticised'. These peoples, who developed a hill-top culture, are identified in the ancient sources as the Gallaeci, Cantabri and Astures. They appear to have been divided into a multitude of smaller tribal communities, whose territory extended little beyond the fortified hill which they inhabited. They were apparently largely static in their cultural and social evolution, retaining many of the customs of the purer Celtic cultures; this was due to their topographical isolation in mountainous and densely wooded terrain. Their area of distribution lay between the

A bronze votary figurine showing a Hispanic warrior in the praying position. Characteristic features of the costume depicted on many of these figurines include short tunics with the waist cinched very tightly by a broad belt: a slim waist was important to the warrior image. (Museo Arqueológico Nacional Madrid)

Cantabrian coast and the basin of the River Durius (Duero).

The central area of Spain, known today as the Meseta or Plateau, comprising the provinces of Salamanca, Caceres, Badajoz and Valladolid and Portugal, was inhabited by peoples who are known today by the conventional name of 'Celt-Iberians', in obvious reference to a fusion of Celtic and Iberian cultures. Their great tribes were the Lusitani, the Vettones, the Vaccei, the Carpetani, the Arevaci and the Pellendones. Each of these tribes had its

[1]See MAA 121, *Armies of the Carthaginian Wars 265–146 BC*

own distinct personality. Under the veneer of Celtic customs they displayed an indigenous identity, due to the higher density of population which existed at the time of the Celtic invasions of the 7th century BC.

The Vaccei, the northernmost group, were distinguishable by a special social structure of collectivist type; this enabled them to exploit successfully the wheat- and grass-growing areas of the western plateau of Spain. In general terms, each tribe was distributed over a whole region in more or less numerous communities, but depending upon a great city which formed its tribal capital, occupying the top of a hill, easily defensible and with good natural water resources nearby. These cities were invariably surrounded by stone walls with strong

towers, enclosing large perimeters within which were several smaller fortified precincts and 'killing grounds'. During the wars with Rome there emerged the practice of gathering more or less the whole tribe within the city, together with their livestock and valuables, producing a considerable increase in population. This practice may explain the existence of the great walled perimeters, intended to offer secure refuge to this additional population.

Another important tribe within the Celt-Iberian group were the Arevaci, a pastoral, sheep-herding people. They maintained their nomadic way of life until finally forced to settle down—and not without great difficulty—by the Romans in the 1st century AD. The Belli and Titii were other Celt-Iberian tribes, who occupied the valley of the River Jalon.

Celt-Iberian social organisation is difficult to discover. Broadly, it seems that ultimate authority was wielded by the council of elders led by the eldest man of the tribe. The council ruled in matters of general practice and law. In time of war, after the necessary deliberations, the command of the fighting men was entrusted to a single military

Found during the summer of 1982, this sculpture shows a young Iberian warrior of the 4th or 3rd century BC in everyday dress rather than war gear. The sculptor has emphasised, for some reason, the manner of holding the forked staff; the hairstyle and earring; and the bridle details—the mount is perhaps only semi-broken, since it appears to have, in addition to the reins, two straps to the breast harness holding the head down. Some symbolic features can also be identified: the horse's front right hoof rests on a severed head, indicating that the rider is a mighty warrior—the Hispanics, like other contemporary cultures, took heads in war. The right rear hoof steps on a bird, indicating the rider's prowess in the hunt. (Luis Canicio; Museo Arqueológico de Jumilla, Murcia)

leader, who was responsible for the conduct of operations and who received full support from the tribe. Usually peaceful, and benign towards strangers, the Celt-Iberians were formidable warriors when menaced or provoked.

The third major grouping, the civilisation of the Iberians, has proved to be one of the most controversial subjects in the study of Spanish protohistory. Some have denied their existence as a true cultural entity; others, with equal vigour, have advanced them as one of the most evolved of the peoples who have formed the mosaic of the Hispanic race.

From the 7th century BC they came under the influences of the Phoenicians, the Greeks, the Egyptians, and all the other Mediterranean cultures. The basic nucleus was formed by the population of the territories associated earlier with the mythical kingdom of Tartessos, and comprising modern Andalusia and the Mediterranean coast, extending up to the southern coasts of France. The Andalusian region had an urban tradition stretching back more than a thousand years, and boasted more than 200 towns. Rich in agriculture and cattle, it also had a fishing industry based on the coastal towns, and, inland, mines producing precious metals. This region was blessed with a benign climate, which favoured all kinds of activities. There was a strong monarchical tradition, the cities being ruled by a king (or, in the term used by the Romans, a *regulus*). Society was complex and stratified; there was a blood aristocracy (Hannibal married an Iberian 'princess'); a class whose prominence depended upon wealth; free citizens; slaves; and a working class, both in public and private employment. With the spread of Roman influence the cities of this region quickly became 'Romanised'; important centres emerged, such as Italica near Seville, where two Roman emperors—Trajan and Hadrian—were born. The more important tribes of this part of Spain were the Turdetani, the Edetani, the Ilergetes and the Contestani.

Social Organisation and Obligations

Celt-Iberian society was organised in basic units which were termed—we have no alternative but to follow the Roman usage—*gentilitates* and *gens*, roughly equivalent to clans and tribes respectively.

Vase paintings of warriors from Liria, dating from the 2nd and 1st centuries BC. The large Celtic *scutum* shields are clearly shown, long spears are carried, and some kind of helmet and body armour is certainly depicted here. Note that the figures at the right of each picture have headgear with 'toothed' or 'cockscomb' crests. Fringing is seen beneath the edge of the short cuirasses, perhaps from the tunic worn beneath the armour. These men seem to wear calf-length boots. (Museo Arqueológico de Valencia)

The smaller community or *gentilitatus* was united by common blood and a common forefather. Within the group individuals enjoyed status through common rights and duties. There were common religious practices; and the territory they inhabited was considered collective property in which each individual had rights. These basic family groups were linked into a more complex group termed by the Romans *gens*; and numbers of these, in their turn, together formed a federation of people.

This society expressed itself through a number of 'political institutions'. Among these was a popular assembly of e.g. the adults of a city, which took decisions on matters of collective importance. A more restricted organ was an assembly of clan leaders or city elders, which under some circumstances could overrule the decisions of the popular assembly. There are various differing references to these forms of government in the written sources. There also existed a form of personal authority wielded by leaders—termed by the Romans as 'kings' or military leaders—who shared power with the assembly and the councils of elders according to some formula. At the time under consideration 'collective power' among the Celt-Iberians was progressively giving way to more restricted forms of power enjoyed by the aristocracy.

The Graeco-Latin sources mention two notable and highly characteristic relationships to be found among the peoples of ancient Spain: in Latin, *fides* and *hospitium*. *Fides* was a broader concept than its simple Latin equivalent suggests; it had an important influence in public and private life, and was also significant in the military context. Among the Iberians the relationship reached a level which has been called *devotio*: the consecration of a man and his relatives to the service of another individual, in return for certain obligations taken on by that individual. This bond between leader and led was sealed with religious invocations, and was of a solemn nature. In this sense it is valid to speak of the creation of 'private armies' around a chieftain or *regulus*; and we may note that the Romans put the local custom to good use by the formation of loyal personal bodyguards of Iberian warriors.

The *hospitium* was a pact, usually reached between clans or *gentilitates*, under which each member of one clan was considered to enjoy full rights and obligations as a member of the other. During a time of warfare these inter-clan obligations were obviously significant.

Contact with the Romans led to the appearance of new social forms, and speeded up the internal processes of social evolution. One result was an extension of private, as opposed to community property; and thus, to the logical appearance of a disinherited class, which chose brigandage, mercenary service under local magnates, or enlistment with the Roman army as a means of subsistence.

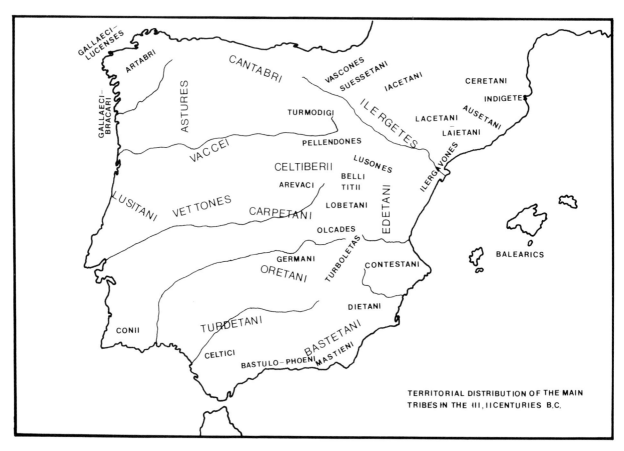

TERRITORIAL DISTRIBUTION OF THE MAIN TRIBES IN THE III, II CENTURIES B.C.

Warfare in Ancient Spain

While it is obviously true that indigence has forced many men—throughout history, and all over the world—to follow the path of the mercenary or the bandit proper, it is no less true that the kind of guerrilla warfare practised by the Hispanic peoples was then considered entirely licit and honourable among some tribes. Diodorus tells us that 'there is a custom characteristic of the Iberians, but particularly of the Lusitans, that when they reach adulthood those men who stand out through their courage and daring provide themselves with weapons, and meet in the mountains. There they form large bands, to ride across Iberia gathering riches through robbery, and they do this with the most complete disdain towards all. For them the harshness of the mountains, and the hard life they lead there, are like their own home; and there they look for refuge, being impregnable to large, heavily equipped armies.' Note that Diodorus speaks here of custom, not of need. These wandering bands rarely attacked members of their own tribes; but, understandably, the Romans were unwilling to grant any colour of honour to their activities, and always referred to them simply as bandits.

There is a ludicrous anecdote which illustrates—albeit by exaggeration—the attitude of these Hispanic warriors to warfare and to life in general. It is said that the Vettones were the first to enlist as mercenaries under the Roman eagles, and to share with legionaries the life of the Roman military camps. One day a group of Vettones, seeing Roman soldiers coming and going about their duties as sentries, became very concerned for them, and tried to take the Romans into their tents: they apparently thought that their new comrades had gone mad from sunstroke, since they could conceive of no other activity between actual fighting, and sitting around at their ease!

Strabo accuses the Iberians of being incapable of forming large confederations, and of dispersing their forces in inter-tribal disputes. This is only true up to a point, since the formation of armies exceeding 100,000 men is recorded[1]. More to the point, there was a general failure to exploit victory

Two bronze votary figurines, showing variations of Hispanic costume. The man on the left is shown with proportions distorted so that the tunic exposes his genitals, doubtless for some ritual reason rather than in literal depiction of the costume. He holds a triangular knife in his right hand; and there appears to be a harness of some kind on his chest, perhaps for the attachment of a breastplate? The right hand figure wears a long garment—a cloak?—and some kind of decoration is visible at the V-neck of his tunic; he holds, or wears slung, a small *caetra* shield. (Museo Arqueológico Nacional, Madrid)

after success in battle. An army's cohesion might be maintained for some time after a victory, however; but in the case of defeat the warriors dispersed very quickly, producing among the Romans the sensation of fighting against an intangible enemy. In set-piece battles on open ground the Romans also suffered the unpleasant surprise produced by Hispanic tactics which differed considerably from the hoplitic methods usual in the Republican Roman army.

After a great deal of preparatory chanting and ritual dancing, the Celt-Iberians would attack *en masse* and in apparent disorder. At a pre-arranged signal the attack was halted, and the warriors would retreat, giving an appearance of defeat. This sequence might be repeated over and over again during several days; and each withdrawal obliged

[1]Though, like all other figures in ancient texts—and like the quoted strengths of armies in this book—this must be regarded with reserve.

the Romans to mount a pursuit, while maintaining their formations. Finally, after several attacks of this kind, it sometimes happened that the Romans lost their discipline—or their nerve—and broke formation to pursue the retreating warriors. At this point the Hispanics would quickly regroup, mounting a counterattack and frequently decimating the legionaries in detail—who, being more heavily equipped and armoured, were less agile in individual combat.

This sort of fighting, known among the Romans as *concursare*, has been described by some as a simple absence of tactics. However, in the present author's opinion there had to be some kind of co-ordination to allow these sudden advances and retreats to occur simultaneously in the confusion of battle, without leaving groups of warriors isolated and outnumbered. It is perhaps relevant here to remark on the frequent archaeological finds throughout Celt-Iberia of rounded horns made of ceramic material, which some believe may have been used to transmit signals in battle.

The use of weapons among the Hispanic male population was varied and widespread; these will be discussed in a later chapter, but it should be noted here that abundant archaeological finds have been made in ancient burials, even in those of men who were evidently of humble means. His weapons were a man's most valuable possessions; and on many occasions we read that negotiations with the Romans were abruptly broken off due to Roman attempts to confiscate weapons.

The Hispanics enjoyed gymnastic exercises; and 'gladiatorial' combats ranged from friendly contests to fights to the death to settle serious differences between warriors. They also practised horsemanship, hunting, and ambushes—indeed, any activity which would qualify them as warriors. Unusually, we learn that it was common for warriors to carry a small receptacle containing a quick-acting poison extracted from the roots of the plant *Ranunculus sardonia* which they used to swallow to give themselves a quick death if all hope was lost. This poison also produced a contraction of the lower jaw, giving the victim the appearance of a sinister—literally, 'sardonic'—smile. This was apparently terrifying to the Roman legionaries, who thought that the dead man was defying them from beyond the grave.

Chronology

First period of conquest, 218–154 BC:

218 BC As a strategic movement in the context of the Second Punic War, two Roman legions commanded by Gnaeus Cornelius Scipio reach the harbour of Cesse (Tarraco)—the first Roman units to set foot on Spanish soil, whose task is to interrupt Carthaginian supplies. Battle of Cesse, capital of the Cessetani.

217 BC The Romans winter in Tarraco, transforming it into a permanent base.

215 BC Publius Cornelius Scipio, brother of Gnaeus, arrives at Tarraco with a troop and supply fleet of 20–30 ships. He defeats the Carthaginians south of the R. Iberus, hindering Hasdrubal's march on Italy. Roman conquest of Saguntum.

212 BC The Scipios are defeated after three years of fighting which saw some Roman territorial gains; Publius is beaten and killed near Castulum (Cazlona) by Hasdrubal, Giscona and Magon, helped by the Ilergetes led by Indibil, a Spanish prince. Gnaeus is defeated, takes refuge in a tower near Ilorci (Lorca?), but is killed by the troops of Hasdrubal Barca. Titus Fonteius saves the rest of the army by leading it to Tarraco.

211 BC Rome sends reinforcements to Hispania under C. Claudius Nero. Publius Cornelius Scipio (later, Africanus), son of the late Publius, arrives invested with the Imperium Praeconsulare and accompanied by M. Junius Silanus.

209–208 BC Indibil of the Ilergetes, Mandonio *regulus* of the Ilergavones and Edecon prince of the Edetani are persuaded to support Scipio. Romans capture Carthago Nova (Carthagena) and gain control of important silver mines; Hasdrubal Barca defeated at Baecula (Bailen) but escapes to Italy.

207 BC Silanus defeats combined Hispano-Carthaginian army led by Magon and Hannon in the Meseta. Scipio's brother Lucius attacks Bastetania and captures Auringis (Jaen), the capital. The Accitani, centred on the capital Acci (Guadix), join the Roman cause.

206 BC Decisive victory for Scipio at Ilipa (Alcala del Rio) Silanus puts Castulum under siege; it is surrendered by Cerdubelo, a Turdetan magnate. Scipio destroys Iliturgi (Mengibar) and retires to Carthago Nova while Silanus and Marcius continue to sack the region. The city of Astapa (Estepa?), loyal to the Carthaginians, is besieged by Marcius; after prolonged resistance the inhabitants commit mass suicide. Gades (Cadiz) surrenders to the Romans. End of the Carthaginian presence in Hispania; the Romans remain as the only foreign troops in the Peninsula. Major uprising in Hispania Citerior[1]. Spanish kings, realising that instead of liberation from Carthaginian oppression they have merely gained new masters, begin war against Rome. Indibil and Mandonio invade territories of the Suessetani and Edetani, allies of Rome; but are defeated by Scipio.

205 BC Renewed uprising in Citerior; but Indibil is defeated and killed, Mandonio captured and executed.

199 BC Spanish cities suffer harsh extortion under proconsuls Cn. Cornelius Vlasius and L. Stertinius.

197 BC C. Sempronius Tuditanis and M. Helvius are sent as governors of

Even this fragment of painted vase, dating from the 1st century BC, shows an interesting detail. The warrior's head, above the painted shield, is protected by a roughly conical helmet drawn up into a spire in the Celtic manner, and fitted with a chinstrap. The wolf's-head symbols are intriguing: the wolf was associated with death in Hispanic religious ritual, and this warrior seems to be surrounded by them. (Museo Arqueológico de Alicante)

Hispania with orders to fix borders between 'Ulterior' and 'Citerior' provinces. Renewed revolt: in Ulterior the Turdetani, led by Culcas and Luxinio, with support from the cities of Sexi (Almuñecar) and Malaca (Málaga), defeat and kill C. Sempronius Tuditanis.

195 BC Consul M. Porcius Cato and praetor P. Manlius are sent to Citerior, Ap. Claudius Nero to Ulterior. Capture of Indika, near Emporion (Ampurias). The Ausetani submit to Cato, as do the Bargusi, whose rebellion ends with Cato taking their capital Bergium (Berga). Edetani submit to P. Manlius. Siege of

[1]Rome divided the occupied territories in Hispania into 'Hispania Citerior' (Nearer Spain) and 'H. Ulterior' (Further Spain), along a border running across the Peninsula roughly from the north-east to the south-west corners. Normally the Senate commissioned a praetor or governor for each province. Hereafter in this text we refer simply to 'Ulterior' and 'Citerior'.

Two more fragments of painted vases of the 2nd-1st centuries BC showing heads protected by two sorts of helmet: the upper one is roughly conical, with neck, cheek, and perhaps even nasal protection, and a buttoned spire; the lower example shows the simple cap-like shape often found in Iberian vase paintings, with a wavy-edged crest. (Museo Arqueológico de Valencia)

Segontia (Segorbe?); submission of Suessetani.

194 BC Cato attacks the Iacetani, helped by the Suessetani, and takes their capital Iacca (Jaca). The Lusitani attack in Ulterior, but are defeated at Ilipa.

193 BC M. Fulvius Nobilior, governor of Ulterior, defeats near Toletum (Toledo) a confederation of Vaccei, Vettones and other tribes.

192–178 BC General uprisings right across the Peninsula; savage fighting.

171 BC Hispanic ambassadors are received by the Senate in Rome to complain about the greed and injustice of Roman governors.

178–154 BC Relative peace in the Peninsula.

Second period of conquest, 155–19 BC:

155–138 BC Lusitan Wars:

155 BC The praetor Manlius is defeated by the Lusitani.

154 BC The praetor Calpurnius Piso is defeated by the Lusitani.

153–151 BC First Numantine War:

153 BC Lucius Mummius, future destroyer of Corinth, named praetor of Ulterior; defeated by Lusitani at Caisaros. Numantia extends protection to the Segetani. Caros defeats Fulvius Nobilior in Citerior. Ambon and Leukon chosen chiefs of the Arevaci by the tribe assembled in Numantia. Celt-Iberians take Roman supply depot at Ocilis (Medinaceli). Nobilior, again beaten by the Numantines, winters in camp on the Gran Atalaya, suffers heavy losses to weather.

(152–143 BC Relative peace in the Meseta)

151 BC L. Licinius Lucullus (the elder) attacks without warning Cauca (Coca) in Vacceian territory and massacres inhabitants; besieges Intercatia (Villalpando) successfully; but fails before Pallantia (Palencia) and retires to Turdetania—territory of pacified tribes.

151–150 BC S. Sulpicius Galba defeated by Lusitani. Under pretext of land distribution he traps, disarms and massacres or enslaves c.10,000 of them, including women and children.

147 BC The praetor Vetilius defeats c.10,000 Lusitani who are attacking Turdetania, trapping them in a valley. Viriatus, elected supreme leader of these forces, leads successful breakout. Vetilius subsequently defeated and killed.

146 BC Viriatus defeats C. Plaucius in Carpetania, takes Segobriga (Saelices), and defeats Claudius Unimanus, governor of Citerior.

145 BC Viriatus' forces defeat C. Nigidius.

144 BC Viriatus, beaten by Q. Fabius

Maximus, evacuates valley of River Baetis (Guadalquivir), retires to Baicor (Baecula?).

143–133 BC Second Numantine War:

143 BC Victories of Q. Caecilius Metellus in Celt-Iberia; Nertobriga (Ricla?), Centobriga and Contrebia submit.

142 BC Metellus attacks the Vaccei during harvest.

141–140 BC Q. Pompeius fails in attacks on Numantia and Termantia. F. Maximus Servilianus sacks towns in Baetica allied to Viriatus; but is later defeated, and signs a treaty. Viriatus receives title *Amicus Populi Romani*—'Friend of the Roman People'. Pompeius fails again before Numantia.

140–139 BC Pompeius concludes treaty with Numantines, imposing tribute of 39 talents of silver. The Senate breaks the peace with Viriatus, and orders Popilius Laenas to resume hostilities against Numantia. Viriatus takes refuge on Mt. Veneris; negotiations with Q. Servilius Cepio; Viriatus assassinated.

138 BC Popilius Laenas' siege of Numantia fails and he withdraws to Jalon valley.

137 BC Numantines defeat consul G. Hostilius Mancinus, who is forced to grant peace terms under shameful conditions. Under pretext that they had helped the Numantines, M. Aemilius Lepidus besieges Vacceian capital of Pallantia. Consul L. Furius Philus of Citerior informs Numantines that the Senate refuses to ratify the peace signed by Mancinus; and attacks the Vaccei.

143–133 BC Consul Publius Cornelius Scipio Aemilianus Africanus[1] leads important Roman reinforcements to Hispania and conducts large scale operations. He attacks the Vaccei to prevent their supporting Numantia; and in October 134 BC begins the siege which finally—in summer 133—brings about the destruction of the city.

132–109 BC Peace in Hispania.

104–103 BC Cimbrians and Teutones invade the Peninsula, but are repulsed by Hispanic armies—to the shame of the praetor Fulvius, who had earlier been defeated by these Celtic invaders.

99 BC New uprising in the Meseta.

Interesting 3rd-century sculpture showing a warrior with a *caetra* slung on a long strap from his shoulders; this strap was apparently wrapped round the forearm in battle. The buckler seems to be shown as made of several layers. The body protection indicated here may be a hardened leather cuirass. Just visible on his right hip (to our left) is the hanging, fringed end of the sash or waistband often depicted; it is thought that different colours may have had some significance in identifying the warrior's status. (Museo Arqueológico de Jaen)

[1]This was the third Publius Cornelius Scipio to fight in Spain; the adoptive grandson of the great Africanus, victor of Ilipa in 206 and over Hannibal at Zama in 202, Scipio Aemilianus was the destroyer of Carthage in 146.

82–72 BC Sertorian Wars, involving Hispanic armies.

61 BC C. Julius Caesar arrives as praetor of Ulterior province.

61–60 BC New campaigns against the Lusitani.

59–57 BC Peace throughout Hispania.

56 BC Revolt of the Vaccei.

49–44 BC War in Spain between Caesar and Pompeius.

39–37 BC Uprising of the Cessetani.

29 BC Campaigns of the legate Estatilius Taurus against the Cantabri, Vaccei and Astures.

28 BC Calvisius Sabinus defeats the Cantabri.

26–25 BC Augustus Caesar takes personal command against the Cantabri; operations against Bergida, Mt.

Vindius and Aracillum. Seriously ill, Augustus retires to Tarraco, passing command to C. Antistius Vetus.

25 BC The Astures, advancing from the hills into the Astura River valley, are forced by the legate P. Carisius to fall back on Lancia (Villasabariego), which falls to the Romans. Emerita Augusta (Mérida) is founded as colony of Roman veterans.

24 BC Augustus returns to Rome, naming Lucius Aemilius as his legate. The Cantabri and Astures break out in rebellion again, but are defeated.

22 BC Renewed hostilities in Cantabria; rebels defeated by combined forces of P. Carisius and C. Furnius.

19 BC Cantabrian prisoners of war, sold as slaves, rebel; they kill their owners and return to the Peninsula, lighting the fire of revolt once again. Augustus sends Agrippa to end this war. The Hispanic L. Cornelius Balbus receives triumphal honours for his African victories—the first non-Italic so honoured.

18 BC Two of the legions which took an active part in the Cantabrian wars, Legio V Alaudae and Legio VIIII Hispana, are transferred to Germany and Illyria respectively—a clear indication that Roman pacification was complete at last, after 200 years of bloody fighting.

A sculpture of a Hispanic warrior which has caused many difficulties of interpretation. The large oval *scutum* shield is quite clear, as is the *falcata* sabre; but the deep, crested headgear is a puzzle. Some authorities associate it with written references to helmets made of animal sinew, but this is not understood. (Museo Arqueológico Nacional, Madrid)

Impact of the Hispanic Wars on Rome

While Rome's first presence in Spain in 218 BC was a strategic move prompted by her need to interfere with a supply base which was allowing Carthaginian forces to press dangerously on Italy, by the aftermath of the battle of Ilipa in 207 or 206 she was already considering indefinite occupation of the Peninsula. Apart from the favourable climate and fertility, which offered a potentially rich source of food supplies for Roman metropolitan areas, the Romans were quick to appreciate the Peninsula's resources of precious and strategic metals: gold, silver, copper and iron. Indeed, the Second Punic War was financed with the silver which the Romans extracted from the mines around Cartagena. As a small example of the exploitation of these resources, Livy lists the following figures. During 200 BC Lentulus removed 43,000 pounds (*libra*) of silver and 2,450 of gold; his colleague Acidinus, 1,200 of silver and 30 of gold.

In 198 BC Cornelius Blasius removed 20,000 pounds of silver, 515 of gold, and 34,500 of coined silver; his colleague L. Stertinius, 50,000 of silver. These sums were realised by pillage and tribute during a time of peace, which perhaps explains the uprising of the following year. In 197 the governor of Hispania Ulterior, M. Helvius, collected 14,732 pounds of silver; 17,023 of coined silver; and 27,000 of *argentum oscensis* (a famous Spanish silver *denarius*, mentioned in this year for the first time). The governor of Hispania Citerior, Q. Minucius, collected 34,800 pounds of silver coined to Iberian designs; 25,000 pounds of unworked silver; 123,000 pounds of silver coined to Roman designs, and 540 pounds of *argentum oscensis*; and 1,400 pounds of gold were amassed by the consul M. Porcius Cato in Citerior in 195 BC. In 192 we read that the praetor of Citerior province, F. Nobilior, collected 12,000 pounds of silver, 130 of coined silver, and 127 of gold. In the year 185 Citerior yielded to the praetor L. Manlius 92 golden crowns and 16,300 pounds of silver, and to the quaestor 10,000 pounds of silver and 80 of gold . . . Examples like these are countless.

The attainment of such riches had a cost: it engulfed Rome in a long and cruel war, which was to have profound effects on the Republic. The bloodshed, and the need to maintain permanent armies in Hispania left a permanent mark. During the 20 years of the Second Celt-Iberian War, 153–133 BC, the Roman population would normally have increased by some 3,000 every year, giving an overall increase of some 60,000. In fact it appears that during these 20 years Rome suffered an overall decrease in population of some 65,000. The losses of her Italian allies were even greater than those among Roman citizens; and it has been estimated that the total losses suffered by Romans and Italians, but excluding other allies, amounted

A 2nd- or 1st-century vase painting from Liria, Valencia, showing a mounted warrior. The headgear resembles a hood; and note the fringes on the trousers or breeches, depicted in a different way from what are apparently fringed tunic hems in other paintings. Note the bell hanging from the horse's throat-lash, and the indication of ornate decoration on its neck and head. (Museo Arqueológico de Valencia)

to between 150,000 and 200,000 during this phase of the Hispanic wars, figures which coincide with certain indications from Roman written sources.

This great expenditure of manpower at times made it impossible to find the necessary troops to maintain operations. During this period there was a property qualification for enlistment as a legionary, of 4,000 as, and this requirement further limited recruitment. Some historians see this as a factor in the proposal of Tiberius Gracchus to reform Roman property law in such a way as to widen the distribution of land holdings, and thus of potential legionaries.

Again, one of the fundamental pillars of the Republican system was the limitation of the period of a senior military command to one year, as a safeguard against military dictatorship. The conditions of the Spanish wars forced the extension of this period, for reasons of efficiency. Public opinion among citizens, and even in the ranks of the army, was by no means solidly behind a war which cost such a price in men and money, as well as introducing these domestic distortions.

Polybius tells us that in 152 BC, when it became necessary to raise an army against the rebellious Hispanic tribes who had inflicted such losses the previous year, there was a general disinclination to accept the burden of military duty, from legate and tribune down to simple legionary; and that this disillusion—and even open fear—continued until the voluntary involvement of the respected Scipio Aemilianus Africanus at the end of these campaigns. The Greek historian also emphasises the extraordinary nature of the fighting in Spain when seen from the standpoint of the classically trained Mediterranean soldier. He called the Spanish war 'the war of fire', not only for its fierceness but for its unpredictability, its alternating outbreaks and periods of smouldering which were never quite stamped out. The Romans, he says, were worn down by the tireless patience of the Hispanics, who could not be beaten quickly in decisive battles, but who stubbornly resisted all day until nightfall brought a temporary end to the fighting, only to return to the fray on the morrow. Even winter did not interrupt the wars in the Peninsula, he writes.

The nature of these centuries of warfare can perhaps be sketched in by recounting in detail two significant episodes: the rebellion of Viriatus, and the Numantine wars.

Iberian warrior and his horse, from another Liria vase painting. Features include the horse's bridle bell and large frontal ornament, saddle, and clearly depicted sex: the latter detail reminds us that however crude the art of some ancient cultures may seem to us, the artists deliberately depicted many details, and we should be cautious in dismissing out of hand features which we find hard to reconcile with our very imperfect knowledge of the time. The warrior here wears a helmet with a crest, and perhaps a rising plume of feathers. (Museo Arqueológico de Valencia)

The Campaigns of Viriatus

The natural obstacles to Rome's conquest and pacification of the Peninsula were aggravated by the ineptitude of many of the military and political leaders entrusted with the task: too often their main aim was the rapid collection of a large personal fortune. The worst rebellions among the tribes were always provoked by the excesses of Roman authorities; and the longest periods of peace coincided with respect shown for the pacts signed between Romans and Hispanics.

In about 151 BC Servius Sulpicius Galba succeeded M. Atilius as praetor or governor of Hispania Ulterior. Newly arrived in Baetica (Andalusia), he ordered his army to march towards Lusitania. After marching 92km in a single journey, his unrested troops were sent straight into action against the Lusitani, who had been causing problems in the region for the past three years. Misled by the tactic of simulated retreat and swift counterattack, some 7,000 out of the force of 15,000 Romans were killed. Galba and the survivors, including his cavalry, took refuge in Carmo (Carmona). At the same time Galba's counterpart in 'Nearer Spain', L. Lucinius Lucullus, was also having difficulty with Lusitan raiders; and he and Galba concerted their operations.

Galba's Massacre

The two forces advanced into Lusitania, pillaging and destroying towns but failing to bring to battle the bulk of the enemy's fighting men. Galba, advised by Lucullus (who also used contemptible methods), then devised a plan for a final solution to the Lusitan problem. Offering to sign a treaty with the Lusitani, he proposed that in return for handing in their weapons they would receive a distribution of farmland. Around 30,000 Lusitani assembled, and were disarmed and separated into three camps. Galba then ordered his troops to massacre the able-bodied men (about 9,000 of them); and sold the rest into slavery. The news of this atrocity caused the governor some difficulties with the Senate when it reached Rome; but its more immediate consequence was one of the worst uprisings Rome ever had to face in Hispania. It was now that the renowned Lusitan hero Viriatus emerged from the shadows of history.

We know that he was of humble origins, perhaps a shepherd. His Romanised name comes from *viria*, meaning bracelet, recalling the popularity of arm-rings among Celt-Iberians. He was famous for his physical prowess and stamina, his sobriety, and his disregard for personal wealth. Diodorus relates a tale of Viriatus' wedding, to the daughter of a rich landowner whom he regarded with some reserve because of his father-in-law's embracing of Roman ways. Remaining unmoved by the dazzling display of gold, silver and colourful fabrics at his wedding feast, Viriatus refused pressing invitations to take a place of honour. He remained standing, leaning on his spear; and took only a little bread and meat, which he shared with his close companions. When the bride was brought before him, he offered sacrifice in the Iberian manner, set her on the crupper of his horse, and rode away into the hills to his hideout.

We know that Viriatus was a survivor of Galba's massacre, and from that day forward implacable in his hatred if the Romans. In 147 BC an army of some 10,000 Lusitani invaded the pacified area of Turdetania. The legate Caius Vetilius managed to encircle the rebels near Urso (Osuna), trapping them in a water-course. Vetilius offered to accept their surrender on the tactless terms of farmland in return for their weapons. Agreement had almost been concluded when Viriatus, a junior chieftain, reminded his countrymen of the discouraging history of such pacts with the Romans. His eloquence moved the tribesmen to hail him as supreme chief on the spot. He selected 1,000 riders, and led them in a diversionary charge on the Romans while the Lusitan footsoldiers un-expectedly broke formation and dispersed. Vetilius hesitated, giving the Lusitani time to withdraw; and Viriatus' horsemen, being lighter and faster than their enemies, managed to fall back in their turn, carrying out a series of hit-and-run attacks over the next few days to cover the retreat of his infantry. Eventually, under cover of night, he finally disengaged and reached Tibola (Baena), rejoining the bulk of his force.

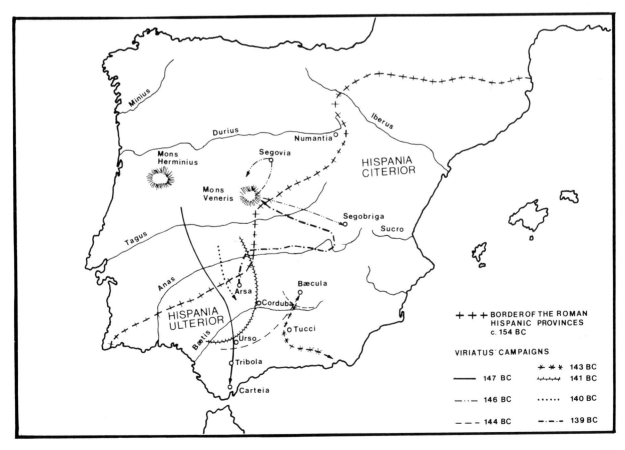

A bronze votary figurine from a sanctuary in Andalusia—ancient Turdetania. The rider wears a close-fitting helmet of the type often depicted. (Museo Arqueológico Nacional, Madrid)

The Death of Vetilius

The praetor, hot to avenge this defeat, then allowed himself to be lured into the narrow pass of the Barbesula (Guadiaro) River valley, which prevented his heavy infantry from deploying. Confident in his numerical superiority, Vetilius was attacked at the far end of the pass, frontally, and on both flanks by Lusitani concealed on the wooded slopes. Neither for the first nor the last time in the Peninsula, a large Roman force allowed itself to be ambushed with serious results. Some 6,000 Romans died, including Vetilius: initially taken alive, he was later cut down, as his captors never imagined that such a fat, elderly man could be an important war leader. (The Hispanic warriors made something of a cult of trim physique, and accentuated the waist by wearing broad, tight belts.)

Vetilius' quaestor took refuge in Carteia (near Gibraltar) with the remaining Roman troops, sending out instead some 5,000 allied Bellian and Titian warriors; these the Lusitani wiped out, as Viriatus was keen to make an example of Hispanics who sided with Rome.

The following year a new praetor, Caius Plaucius, brought to the Peninsula reinforcements of some 10,000 foot and 1,300 horse; more could not be found, since Rome was then heavily committed to the Third Punic War with Carthage. Viriatus, who was harrassing the Carpetan territories, ambushed and wiped out some 4,000 Romans sent against him by Plaucius. Plaucius followed the Lusitani to their refuges around Mt. Veneris, but was again beaten, and was forced to withdraw earlier in the season than usual to winter quarters. This left Viriatus with the initiative; he exploited it in a series of attacks on Roman garrisons in central Hispania which caused much damage, not least to Roman morale.

His next move was towards Segobriga (near Cuenca), in order to promote alliances with the Celt-Iberian kingdoms in that area. Claudius Unimanus—possibly the praetor of Citerior—led a major force out in an attempt to avenge his colleague's defeat; but was beaten in his turn, in a disaster which cost many lives and much booty—the latter, including standards, being displayed publicly all through the mountain country on Viriatus' orders. Unimanus himself paid tribute to Hispanic spirit: '. . . In a narrow pass 300 Lusitani faced 1,000 Romans; as a result of the action 70 of the former and 320 of the latter died. When the victorious Lusitani retired and dispersed confidently, one of them on foot became separated, and was surrounded by a detachment of pursuing cavalry. The lone warrior pierced the horse of one of the riders with his spear, and with a blow of his sword cut off the Roman's head, producing such terror among the others that they prudently retired, under his arrogant and contemptuous gaze . . .'

Viriatus proceeded to capture Segobriga by a ruse, surprising the inhabitants—who had not joined the Lusitan cause—by a simulated retreat and a forced march. This period marked the peak of his success; after smashing several Roman armies he had acquired great prestige throughout the country, and men flocked to join him. But with the war against Carthage finally concluded, Rome was free to concentrate on the Lusitani.

Fabius' Campaigns

In 145 BC the great consul Publius Cornelius Scipio Aemilianus Africanus entrusted his brother Q. Fabius Maximus with Ulterior and his friend C. Laelius with Citerior. Africa and Macedonia were still absorbing large Roman forces, and the Senate only provided Scipio with an army of 15,000 legionary recruits, 2,000 horse and ten war elephants: a small field army to safeguard both Hispanic provinces, though sufficient to protect the occupied towns. Fabius concentrated his recruits at Urso (Osuna); he spent a year training his men, ignoring the harassing attacks of the Lusitani and Viriatus' attempts to provoke him into taking the field. He also made every effort to secure more local co-operation, sailing to Cadiz to take part in solemn religious rituals to this end.

Finally, in 144 BC, Fabius passed on to the offensive after three years during which Lusitan command of the countryside had been almost unchallenged. In the first engagement Viriatus was beaten, with heavy loss, and was forced to winter in Cordoba. This first Roman victory since 153 BC gave the Romans a brief respite, and they recovered some key towns. In 143 Viriatus managed to associate the Arevaci, Belli and Titii with his movement; and thus began the Numantine War, which lasted for ten years.

During 143–142 BC renewed operations against the governor of Citerior, Q. Pompeius, caused further Roman reverses; the recapture of Itucci (Martos) gave the rebels domination of the whole Baetic region. Rome decided to send to Hispania another consul from the prestigious Scipio family: Q. Fabius Maximus Servilianus, an adoptive brother of Q. Fabius Maximus, with an army of 18,000 infantry (based on two incomplete legions) and 1,600 horse. His attempt to dislodge Viriatus from Itucci failed; and the Lusitan counterattack led to an indecisive battle between about 6,000 men on each side. Servilianus received from Africa a reinforcement of 300 Numidian horse and ten elephants; he constructed a strong forward base camp, and in a subsequent engagement inflicted a defeat on the Lusitani.

In the course of 140 BC Roman fortunes faltered once more; Viriatus avoided pitched battles and followed his classic hit-and-run tactics with some success. In at least one action they worked to

General view of the famous 'vase of the armoured Warriors' from Liria; note that all these figures wear similar, but not identical armour, and the kind of variations which we would expect in ancient times are clearly indicated. The warrior on the left wears a full corselet of what is clearly intended to be scale armour; if we may interpret the cross-hatched convention as indicating ring mail, which seems logical, then the warrior on the right has a full mail shirt, and the centre figure a mixed corselet with scale on the upper torso and mail on the abdomen. All wear cap-like Iberian helmets, in two cases apparently faced with scale protection, and with wavy-edged crests. All carry the *scutum* and spears. (Museo Arqueológico de Valencia)

perfection; the Romans were provoked into a disorderly pursuit, losing 3,000 men to the lightning enemy counterattack. The subsequent Lusitan attack on the Roman camp caused panic, and legionaries even deserted their defences to seek safety among the tent lines; Servilianus and his tribunes, reimposing discipline with great difficulty, only averted disaster through the heroism of an officer named Fannius (the son-in-law of C. Laelius), and through the coming of nightfall: the Lusitani did not like fighting at night, for religious reasons.

However, the long years of war had caused a steady attrition of Viriatus' strength; and he decided to destroy his camps in central Hispania and to withdraw to the Lusitan heartland to build up reinforcements. Servilianus took advantage of this phase to recapture five towns which had allied with Viriatus—among them Tucci, Astigi and Obulco—and to pacify the Baetic region. The Romans treated their prisoners cruelly, beheading 500 of the 10,000 captured and selling the rest into slavery. They then advanced on Lusitania. On the march they were attacked by some 10,000 men, apparently led by two Roman deserters, Curius and Apuleius. In a fierce and confused action the former was killed, but the Romans temporarily lost their baggage train.

Servilianus now laid siege to a town called Erisana. Viriatus entered the city by audaciously attacking a force of Roman sappers who were undermining the walls by night; they fled, leaving their tools. Attacking the bulk of the Roman force, from inside the city, Viriatus penned them in a narrow pass; and then, incomprehensibly, offered them peace terms. He demanded only that the borders of Lusitania itself should be respected, and that the tribe be granted the status of *amici populi Romani*—'Friends of the Roman People', or independent allies. Servilianus accepted these terms, which were ratified by the Senate.

That a leader so implacably hostile should have concluded this pact with Rome is surprising; possibly Viriatus was becoming tired after so many years of war. In any event, the pact did not last.

An enlarged detail from the Liria vase, showing the figure apparently wearing a corselet of mixed construction. The motifs on the *scutum* recall the flowing patterns of more northerly Celtic peoples, emphasising that it is dangerous to treat too rigidly the division of Hispanic peoples into cultural areas. The spear may represent a *soliferrum*. (Museo Arqueológico de Valencia)

Viriatus was still considered a dangerous focus of resistance, and Rome subsequently ordered her governors in Hispania to get rid of him by any convenient means: he had humiliated Roman pride, and his domination of the wealthy Baetic area was unacceptable. In 140 BC there arrived in Hispania the consul Q. Servilius Cepio, brother of Servilianus, with instructions to break the peace. While he launched a series of increasingly open provocations against the Lusitani, Popilius Laenas began following the same tactic in Celt-Iberia.

The Death of Viriatus
Cepio recaptured Erisana by a sudden stroke. Surprised, Viriatus was forced to abandon the towns of the Baetic area and to retire into Carpetania. Cepio almost trapped him there, but he managed to escape, though much depleted, and returned to Lusitania. Cepio followed him across the territory of the Vettones, allies of the Lusitani, and for the first time entered the mountainous country of the Gallaeci. He constructed a road from the Anas (Guadiana) River to the Tagus (Tajo), and established a great camp, Castra Servilia, near Caceres. Exploiting a period of relative calm in Celt-Iberia, Popilius Laenas joined Cepio in attacking the Lusitani on two fronts. Cepio's advance failed due largely to a mutiny among his cavalry, provoked by his harshness. Meanwhile the Lusitani, exhausted by war, asked Viriatus to negotiate with P. Laenas, who was Cepio's superior.

The Roman general presented to Viriatus his terms: the surrender of Roman deserters, and the handing in of weapons. The first was agreed, and these unfortunates suffered the amputation of their right hands—a punishment in fact learned from the Hispanics. The second, as always, was resisted; but, pressed by his countrymen, Viriatus sent three comrades—Audax, Ditalco and Minuros—to pursue negotiations with Cepio. During these meetings the Romans bribed the three to murder their leader. Appian recounts that Viriatus, who slept little and always in full armour in case of emergency, was stabbed during the night in his tent; the wound was in his neck, the only unprotected part, and was so small that it went unnoticed for some time—his attendants thought he was asleep. This gave the assassins a chance to slip back to the Roman camp to demand their pay. Cepio let them keep what they had received in advance; for the rest, he passed their request to Rome. The Senate replied laconically that Rome did not pay traitors. Thus the great leader of the Lusitani perished, by treachery compounded with treachery.

Desolated by his death, Viriatus' countrymen celebrated extraordinary funeral rites for him. A warrior named Tantalus tried to continue the rebellion, attacking Cartagena without success; but without the inspiring genius of Viriatus the Lusitani were soon obliged to lay down their arms. Servilius Cepio in fact treated them with more mercy than had Laenas; farmland was indeed distributed, the better shares going to those who had submitted to Rome earliest. Some groups were deported and established in other regions—Valencia is supposed to have been founded by one such group.

The Numantine Wars

When, in late summer 133 BC, the gates of the smouldering city of Numantia opened and a staggering crowd of human ghosts emerged to surrender to a Roman army, the moment marked the end of a ten-year war which had cost Rome unbearable humiliations.

The first contact between Numantia and the Romans is thought to have taken place in 197, when the consul Cato was forced by a dangerous outbreak in central Hispania to make the first incursion into the Plateau—Meseta—region, though with little success. Repulsed before Segontia (Sigüenza), he marched with seven cohorts towards the Ebro River; and established camps on a mountain some 6km from Numantia, called today La Gran Atalaya—'the great watchtower'. The site of the base he set up there was to be used by all his successors in their operations against Numantia. Although the record is uncertain, it is not thought that any other Roman general ventured so deep into Celt-Iberia until 153 BC.

After decades of ignored complaints about the rapacity of Roman authorities in Hispania the main towns of Celt-Iberia, such as Segeda (near Zaragoza?), the capital of the Belli, decided to prepare themselves for war. Led by the chieftain Caros, they began to enlarge and repair the walls of the city; and the inhabitants of neighbouring villages, including those of the nearby Titii, were forced to take shelter in the strengthened fortress. Roman protests, and attempts to recruit auxiliaries for the war against the Lusitani, were rejected. At this time the Lusitani frequently displayed before the Celt-Iberians the weapons, standards and other booty they had captured from the Romans; and mocked them for their passivity.

Rome, foreseeing a hard fight, raised a 30,000-strong consular army instead of the more common praetorian army of around 10,000 to 15,000. Command was entrusted to Q. Fulvius Nobilior, a man of aristocratic lineage whose father had combat experience in Hispania in the 190s, but who proved to have learned little from the example. Nobilior's commission was signed before the actual outbreak of war; and according to the usual practice he should have taken command of his army on 15 March 153 BC, at the start of the official year. This would mean that operations could not get under way until June; and, since the weather turns bad in Celt-Iberia in September, this would leave an unrealistically short campaigning season. It was therefore decided in Rome to change the start of the official year to 1 January: we owe the date of our New Year to the Celt-Iberian war.

Nobilior arrived at Tarraco in April, and in May

Drawing of another figure from the 2nd/1st century Liria vase, showing, perhaps, an Iberian officer—this is the only figure which wears this type of large-crested helmet. He holds a clearly-depicted *falcata* and a spear, and his corselet is of scale armour. (Author's drawing)

he advanced on Segeda by following the Ebro up to Zaragoza, and then taking the River Jalon valley. He arrived before the city in June with 30,000 men: two Roman citizen legions each of 5,000, 10,000 allied Italians, 2,400 Roman cavalry, and some 7,000 Hispanic auxiliaries recruited around Tarraco. The Belli and Titii could oppose this army with only 8,000 warriors; and the walls of the city were still not complete. It was therefore decided to abandon Segeda and escape to the territories of allied tribes along the Duero River. Numantia, the most influential centre in the region, accepted the fugitives and agreed to take the brunt of the war.

A collection of Hispanic knives of the type known as 'triangulars'. Note the 'atrophied antennae' pommel shape also found on Hispanic straight swords of the period. These weapons remind us that the Romans copied Hispanic daggers as well as swords: the evolution of the classic Roman legionary dagger, which remained in use for centuries, can clearly be seen here. (Author's drawing)

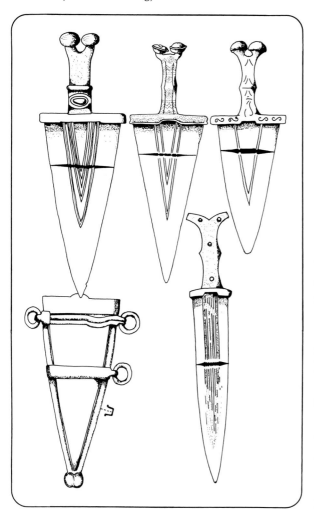

Destroying Segeda, Nobillior continued his march along the Jalon. He organised and garrisoned a supply depot at Ocilis (Medinaceli), on an easily defended hill (though, since it was isolated in the heart of enemy territory, it was not surprisingly lost after the first Roman defeats in this campaign). He drew near to Numantia, where the tribesmen were concentrated. A Numantine embassy interceding for the people of Segeda was rejected, with the demand that all weapons be handed over. This demand was rejected in its turn by the Numantines, who now counted some 25,000 men in their combined army.

Nobilior probably foresaw a classic clash of armies on open ground, but he was disappointed: it is no accident that even today the world 'guerrilla' is written in Spanish the world over. The Roman column began a four-day, 80km march from Ocilis to Numantia across the plateau between the rivers Duero and Jalon. At Ribarroya, 20km from Numantia, they left the Duero and entered the valley of a tributary, the Baldano, in search of a shortcut. In summer this is a completely dry track about 4km long, densely wooded on each side. Here Caros, leading the confederated tribes, had concealed up to 20,000 foot and 5,000 horse; and here Nobilior neglected proper reconnaissance, and led his army into the trap strung out in a long column. In the massive ambush which closed upon them some 10,000 Roman troops fell. The date was 23 August, the day when Rome celebrated the feast of Vulcan. (When news of the disaster reached Rome that date was declared *dies ater*, 'a sinister day', and ever afterwards no Roman general would willingly accept battle on 23 August.) After suffering heavy casualties Nobilior's column hacked its way free and reached open ground. The infantry took up close formation; and the cavalry were able to deploy successfully, killing many Celt-Iberian foot soldiers and their chieftain Caros. It took Nobilior two days to resume his march.

On the Gran Atalaya he ordered the construction of a large camp on the remains of those built by Cato. He received reinforcements of ten elephants and 300 Numidian horse; but by now the garrison of Numantia had also been strengthened, and was once more around 25,000 strong. In September 153 Nobilior attacked the city, relying heavily on the surprise his elephants would

A fine example of the Hispanic straight sword, showing characteristic features: the 'atrophied antennae' pommel, and the three hanging-rings on the scabbard. Both scabbard and hilt are richly inlaid with silver; such expensively decorated examples are relatively common among archeological finds, even in the burials of men of apparently quite humble means.

produce. In an encounter on the grassy slope east of the city he successfully panicked the Numantines by the sudden revelation of this 'secret weapon', and advanced on their heels to the very walls of Numantia. Fortune seemed to be smiling on the Romans, when a freak incident robbed them of victory. A large stone thrown from the walls struck one of the elephants and it ran amock, stampeding the others. As the maddened beasts raged through their ranks the Roman soldiers gave way in confusion; the garrison made a timely sortie, and the day ended with 4,000 Romans and three elephants dead, at a cost of 2,000 Numantine lives.

Nobilior continued to carry out minor operations in the area, but the only result was a steady attrition of his forces. Ocilis fell, and with it went Nobilior's freedom of manoeuvre. With his remaining 5,000 men he decided to winter in the camp on the Gran Atalaya; and over the coming months there his army was further reduced by cold, famine and sickness.

This unfortunate campaign was typical of several other Roman attempts on the Numantine area. In his day Q. Calpurnius Piso had flatly refused to attack the city. In 152, the year after Nobilior's fiasco, there was an unsuccessful attempt under Marcellus; in 151, by Lucullus; in 143, by Metellus and Pompeius; in 138, by Popilius Laenas; in 137 by Mancinus—when a Roman army of some 20,000 was trapped and forced to accept terms by some 4,000 Numantines; and in 136, by Lepidus and Furius Philus.

This series of humiliations finally provoked Rome into sending to Hispania probably her finest living soldier: Publius Cornelius Scipio Aemilianus Africanus, grandson of the victor over Hannibal, and himself the destroyer of Carthage in the Third Punic War. The Senate waived the legal ban on any man holding two consulships within ten years, and he was given the 'extraordinary' appointment as consul of Hispania Citerior for 134 BC. He was not, however, given an army of a size commensurate with his rank, and was only allowed to raise volunteers. The Asian kings Antiochus Sidetes and Atalus III of Pergamon both contributed money to the enterprise; and joined, with other friends and clients, a volunteer *cohors amicorum* to accompany him. This unit included in its ranks several men destined to become famous in their own right: among them, Gaius Marius, Jugurtha, Gaius Gracchus, the historian Polybius, the poet Lucilius, Scipio's brother Q. Fabius Maximus, and Q. F. Buteus, who was charged with leading the troops to the Peninsula.

Landing at Tarraco in March 134, Scipio found the 20,000-strong army commanded by G. Hostilius Mancinus in a lamentable condition. Defeats, uncertainties, frequent changes of command, the effects of the previous winter, and now the nearby delights of a wealthy port and city had caused a major breakdown of morale and discipline.

Camp-followers and hangers-on were driven from the camps; luxuries were forbidden, and personal baggage was reduced to a minimum, along with transport facilities. Dress and rations were reduced to austere levels; Scipio set an example by adopting, and ordering for all personnel, the rough wool *sagum* worn by the Hispanic tribesmen in the country where they would be fighting. He instituted an intense training programme of drills, route marches, and practice fortifications and assaults.

On the march the general made a point of bringing up the rear of the column, indicating his suspicion that too many legionaries were ready to drop out at the first opportunity. Each man was ordered to carry a month's wheat ration, and no less than seven rampart stakes. Physical punishment with the officers' vine sticks was reintroduced for all offenders, including Roman citizens. Significantly, much attention was paid to reconnaissance tactics.

In May of 134 BC Scipio began his march in the direction of Numantia, choosing the longest route (approximately that of the modern Burgos-Logroño road). This route avoided some of the worst 'ambush country'; and also allowed him to harass the territories of the Vaccei, commandeering their crops for his army's use, and discouraging any support they might be contemplating giving the Numantines. The first encounter came at Tierra de Campos, when Vacceian tribesmen attacked Romans who were cutting their wheat; an inexperienced tribune, Rutilius Rufus, led four cavalry squadrons into an ambush when he reacted to this attack. Marching at night to escape the intense heat and thirst of the day, the army pushed on toward Cauca; however, their driven livestock suffered badly. Another ambush in the Guadar-rama valley was fought off without serious loss. Finally, Scipio arrived before Numantia in late

August or early September. Here he met up with Jugurtha, who supplied several war elephants with 'turret crews' of slingers and archers.

By now his total forces numbered about 60,000 men. He had brought 4,000 with him from Italy, and these he kept under his personal command. The numerous submitted Iberian kingdoms of the Ebro valley, the Belli and the Titii provided some 5,000. Of the main army of 20,000 men, 10,000 were Roman and Italian troops and 10,000 were auxiliaries. Scipio thus had 14,000 completely reliable men; but he had less than perfect confidence in the rest.

The Siege

Numantia was on top of a hill, 1,074m above sea level, known today as Muela de Garray, some 9km north of Soria. The Rivers Duero and Merdancho protect the hill from the south-west and west; and on the northern side a tributary flowing into the Duero creates an area of small lakes. A slope to the north-east is the only practical approach for an attacking army. Across the Duero to the west and south stand hills of about the same elevation as Numantia, offering good observation and blockade positions.

Archaeology suggests that the city would have extended over some 22 hectares (1ha = 2.47 acres), the main axes measuring 720m and 310m. In its 2,000 houses lived nearly 10,000 persons; calculating at one man capable of bearing arms to each

Three-view drawing of a *caetra* buckler; note the very substantial handgrip, which is characteristic of these shields, and the rings for the slinging strap. (Author's drawing)

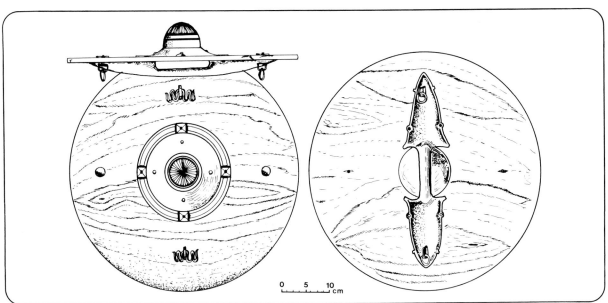

0   5   10
cm

household of four, we arrive at an effective garrison of c.2,500 warriors. To this we may add c.1,000 warriors who probably came in to shelter in the city from the outlying villages, giving c.3,500—or about one-twentieth the Roman strength.

Few remains survive of what were once strong defensive walls surrounding at least three roughly concentric fortified precincts at different levels, walls strengthened by large square towers with a diameter of about 5.7m. When Scipio arrived the walls were partly demolished on the southern and western sides, though here the defenders had thrown up improvised fortifications with stakes, pointed stones and ditches.

It may be thought surprising that Scipio did not launch an immediate assault, in view of his numerical superiority. However, he did not have complete confidence in much of his army; and the respect inspired by the Numantines in previous campaigns was not to be taken lightly. Polybius, who was an eyewitness, writes that Scipio '. . . did not consider it reasonable to engage desperate men, but preferred rather to encircle them and starve them into surrender . . .'

Scipio's first step was to raise an initial palisade around the vulnerable north-east sector of the city's approaches: the rivers, in autumn flood, made a good enough obstacle on the west and south. The pallisade, reinforced with stones and earth and by a half-metre ditch with pointed stakes at the bottom, took some 16,000 stakes and stretched some 4,000m; in view of the relatively treeless terrain, Scipio's foresight in loading his men with stakes was vindicated. The palisade was raised in a single day; this rapidity shocked the Numantines, but they quickly recovered and mounted sorties against the Romans. Although Scipio had enough men to mount strong guards over the working gangs, it seems that Numantine attacks caused serious panic on at least one occasion.

Next, with the provisional palisade completed, Scipio began the construction—100m behind it—of the true 'wall of circumvallation': one of those awesomely thorough, patient feats of military engineering which explain Rome's mastery of the world. It was a stone wall, 4m thick at the base and 2.4m at the top, 3m high from ground to rampart-walk, defended on the inside by a V-section ditch 3m deep. When complete it is thought to have

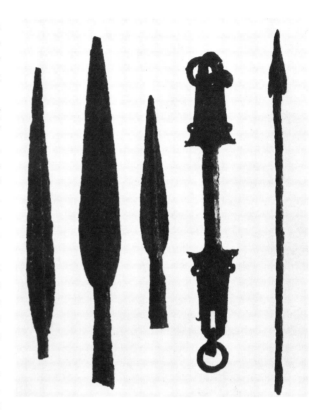

Three excavated iron spearheads of various sizes; the handgrip from a *caetra*; and part of a *soliferrum*, showing its barbed head.

stretched nearly 9km—double the perimeter of Numantia itself. Every 30.85m (the interval called a *plethron*) there was a square, four-storey wooden tower on a base measuring 4m × 5m, the upper floors for sentries and signalling, the lower for war machines. In each of the 300 towers was at least one catapult—more than 400 in all—throwing balls of 1 or 2lbs weight or shooting bolts, over ranges of around 300m[1]: Frederick the Great's artillery did not have much greater range than that of Scipio. These light catapults were supported by 50 heavy *ballistae* or stone-throwers emplaced in the various camps, to bombard the walls and visible concentrations of the defenders. The missiles they threw were normally of about 10lbs weight, judging by those found on the site of the city; but at Caceres balls of stone weighing from 27lbs to 76lbs have been found; and there even existed some weighing three talents or 156lbs—the heaviest 'calibre' known.

[1]As verified by the experimental reconstructions of Gen. Schramm in the years before the outbreak of World War I; see also Paul Holder, *Roman Artillery*, Military Illustrated magazine Nos. 2 and 4, Aug. and Dec. 1986.

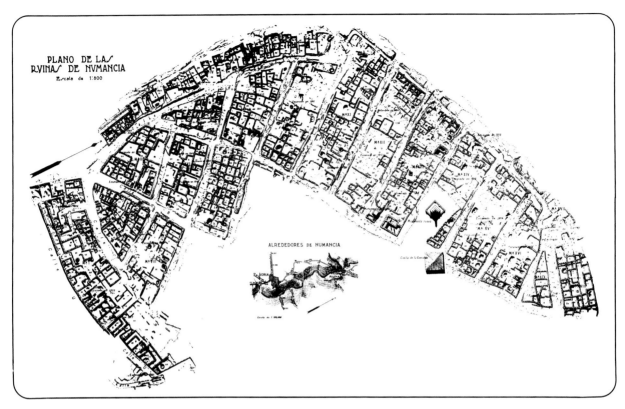

PLANO DE LAS
RVINAS DE NVMANCIA
Escala de 1:800

ALREDEDORES DE NUMANCIA

Plan of the excavated ruins of Numantia.

To support the construction of the wall of circumvallation two camps were built, diametrically opposite one another, and in permanent communication by red flag signals during daylight and by lantern signals at night. The first was that known today as Castillejo, 1km north of Numantia on a hill at whose base runs the River Tera. The visible remains correspond to the last of three camps built there at various dates. Scipio established his headquarters here during the siege, and one of the most important archaeological finds was the floor of his *praetorium*. Its characteristics correspond with those of a Greek-style peristyle house of some luxury. Here lived Scipio, with some 300 other Roman notables; and the camp held 2,500 men (able to be doubled in case of need) as a permanent garrison.

Some 600m to the south-east of the city, on a sharp spur of a hill above the River Merdancho a few yards from its confluence with the Duero, lay the camp of Peñarredonda, well fortified and exploiting the favourable topography. The orderly pattern of streets and buildings suggests a garrison of legionaries, with cavalry lines, tribunes' houses,

and batteries of *ballistae*. This camp has been calculated, from its area of about 11ha, as holding some 5,200 men; it was under the direct command of Scipio's brother, Q. Fabius Maximus. Together Castillejo and Peñarredonda (or Peña Redonda) constituted an axis of vigilance and defence, necessary at first to safeguard the work of the men constructing the lines of circumvallation from enemy interference. From these two dominant positions the walls spread out right and left, creeping across the landscape until they linked up in a continuous belt around Numantia.

To the east of Peñarredonda, on a flat-topped hill called Valdevorron, lie the remains of a camp of some 9ha, large enough for 1,000 men, and still showing the base for a battery of four *ballistae*. Further to the north, on flat ground, are the remains of Traveseras camp, 4ha in extent, with praetorian gates and turreted inner defences. At this point the wall swings inwards towards Castillejo. West of that camp it follows a bend of the River Tera, then continues south on its right bank until it crosses the Duero just above its confluence with the Tera. South of the crossing lies Alto Real camp, with surviving signs of parallel walls, and rooms excavated from the rock. South-west of this is a hill

120

Iberian chieftain, lady, and warrior
of late 3rd/early 2nd century BC.

A

Iberian warriors, late 2nd C. BC;
see Plates commentaries for details.

B

1, 2: Hispanic cavalrymen, 2nd C. BC
3: Roman citizen *equites*, 2nd C. BC

C

Hispanic warriors, 2nd C. BC;
see Plates commentaries for details.

D

1: Andalusian warrior, 2nd C. BC
2, 3: Balearic slingers, 2nd C. BC

F

Celt-Iberian warriors, c.150 BC;
see Plates commentaries for details.

G

Celt-Iberian warriors, c.130 BC;
see Plates commentaries for details.

today called Dehesilla, overlooking the Duero, which is topped with robust walls 4m thick. Finally, due south of Numantia, lay the seventh camp of La Rasa, defending the heights between the Duero and Peñarredonda and some 6ha in extent, with a perimeter of 300m and two protected gateways. The Roman lines are intelligently sited on the topographical features, enclosing the city completely at a range mostly between 100m and 300m, well within range of the Roman artillery. Only opposite the north-east sector does the 'no man's land' widen to c.500m, and on this face the lack of natural protection made this wide space advisable for the sake of observation and ample warning of attack. Since the Numantines were not archers, but spearmen and slingers, with a maximum range of 50 and 100m respectively, they were unable to harass the Roman positions without leaving the protection of the walls of the city.

At one point, apparently, a lake about 700m wide interrupted the circumvallation; here the Romans constructed a dam 100m wide, across which the wall was continued. The rivers interrupted the line at four points; at three of them—the Tera, north and south, and the Merdancho—there were bridges, but at the Duero crossing the Romans had great difficulty, as the stream itself was 80m wide, and its sloping banks added another 60m to the valley. The abutments of the bridge which Scipio tried to construct here can still be seen. According to Appian, these weak points in the circumvallation were exploited by the Celt-Iberians, who brought men and supplies into the city by means of rowing and sailing boats. To prevent this Scipio ordered the construction of booms of wooden beams bristling with iron spikes, with one end moored to the banks and the other floating free; two forts were also built to cover these points, north and south of the city.

Appian records the distribution of the Roman army throughout this formidable siege system. 30,000 men were quartered in the camps, and the other 30,000 along the walls. As the camps were the supporting or reserve bases, the 14,000 Roman and Italian troops were posted in the main camps and the Iberians, stiffened with a nucleus of Italians, in the secondary camps. Some 20,000 men served on the wall itself, and 10,000 were held some way behind it, divided into units of even strength, ready

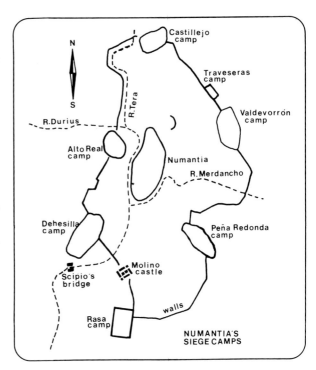

Plan of the formidable siege system constructed by the Romans around Numantia in 134 BC, based on seven camps. (**Author's drawing**)

to support any point on the perimeter in case of danger. These units lived in houses constructed in the local manner. Numantine houses had two floors, one at ground level and one dug down into the ground under its wooden floor, thus enjoying insulation from the extremes of temperature. If we discount from the perimeter the 2,500m covered by the camps themselves, the remainder was held by about four men for every metre; the camp garrisons may be considered as the general reserve and the units outside the wall as the sector reserve.

The line of blockade was an active organism, thanks to the sophisticated communications system employed. In case of daytime attack from the Numantines, a red flag tied to a long spear was raised at the threatened point; at night some kind of lantern or torch signal was displayed. The alarm trumpets were immediately blown, the wall garrison took their battle positions, and the sector and general reserves were alerted. At the same time an officer hastened from the threatened point to the nearest camp or headquarters to report and to receive orders. The red flag signals, apparently used here for the first time, are attributed to the initiative of Polybius himself.

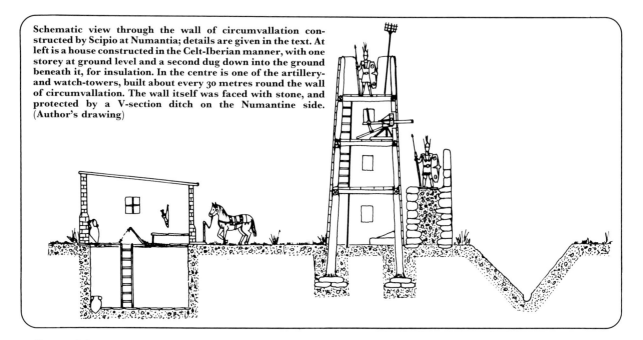

Schematic view through the wall of circumvallation constructed by Scipio at Numantia; details are given in the text. At left is a house constructed in the Celt-Iberian manner, with one storey at ground level and a second dug down into the ground beneath it, for insulation. In the centre is one of the artillery- and watch-towers, built about every 30 metres round the wall of circumvallation. The wall itself was faced with stone, and protected by a V-section ditch on the Numantine side. (Author's drawing)

So confident were the Romans in their defensive system that Titus Livius records that orders were given not to interfere with Numantines spotted searching for firewood and water in the 'no man's land' between the two walls, in order to encourage them to use up these resources as quickly as possible. The work of circumvallation was completed by November 134 BC, and Scipio settled down to starve the Numantines out. He toured the whole perimeter daily, to keep his men alert. The 3,000 or so Numantines did not remain passive, but launched repeated attacks on different sectors of the circumvallation, covering these sorties with diversionary attacks elsewhere; but with their limited numbers, these attempts must have stretched their manpower to the utmost. They also attempted to lure the Romans into open battle; but Scipio, against the urging of his officers, refused to rise to the bait. The only result of these attacks was to wear down the strength of the Numantines.

With the situation inside the city deteriorating, as supplies became exhausted and all hope of outside help was abandoned, a noted citizen named Retogenes Caraunios made a last desperate attempt to summon assistance. One dark night, with five friends and five servants, he climbed the Roman wall by means of a rope ladder, killed the sentries, and—with five companions—managed to seize horses and ride for help, the others returning to the city. He rode to a number of Vacceian towns, appealing for help; but, for fear of Roman reprisals, he was refused by all except the citizens of Lutia (Cantalucia). There some 400 young warriors agreed to come to the aid of Numantia. Their decision was taken against the advice of the council of elders, who, to avert Roman reprisals, sent word to Scipio's camp. Receiving the intelligence at 2 p.m., Scipio marched immediately for Lutia at the head of a punitive column of light troops. At dusk the next day the Romans surrounded the town, and demanded the surrender of the volunteers. They had already fled with Retogenes; but when the citizens told him of this, Scipio retorted that if the guilty parties were not given up, he would allow his troops to sack the town. In the face of this threat the Lutians surrendered 400 innocent youths, who suffered the amputation of their right hands. Next morning Scipio was back on the walls before Numantia.

With this collapse of the last desperate effort to bring help to the besieged city, the starving Numantines, in spring 133 BC, sent an embassy of five men, led by one Avaro, to negotiate terms with Scipio. The Roman general, who was well aware of the state of the garrison from questioning prisoners, demanded unconditional surrender and the confiscation of all weapons. As on previous occasions, this last was enough to bring talks to a halt, since the Hispanic warrior regarded the giving up of his weapons as the ultimate shame. When the embassy returned to the city and repeated Scipio's terms, Celt-Iberian arrogance reached its paroxysm. The messengers were accused of treacherously dealing with the Romans for their own personal benefit, and were butchered on the spot—to be a messenger in the ancient world was not an enviable appointment . . .

Stark starvation now faced the townspeople; bread, meat, and animal forage had all been exhausted, and the survivors were passing from eating the boiled hides of animals to outright cannibalism: first of the dead, then of the ill, and finally of the weak. There are numerous classical accounts of the last days of Numantia. Valerius Maximus says of the Numantine Theogenes: '. . . Only the fierceness of his race could give such vigour of mind. Being superior to all others in honours, dignity and wealth, when the cause of the Numantines was lost, [he] placed firewood everywhere and set fire to his houses, which were the most beautiful in the city. Then he appeared before his fellow citizens, naked sword in hand, and forced them to fight each other in pairs: the vanquished being thrown, after decapitation, into the fires. When all others had submitted to this terrible death-law, he threw himself into the flames . . .' This attitude seems to have been general, as Florus wrote: 'The Numantines, possessed of the most furious rage, determined to take their own lives, destroying themselves, their leaders and their homeland by iron, poison, and the fires that they set everywhere. Only when all human courage was exhausted did [the survivors] decide to surrender.'

Scipio ordered them to deposit their weapons in an agreed place, and for the survivors of the holocaust to congregate at another spot on the following day. When the Numantines asked for one more day, it was granted; and in this interval many more of them, reaching a climax of desperation, committed suicide rather than endure the fall of their city. The next day they surrendered their weapons, and on the third day the last survivors gave themselves up. The Romans watched as they staggered from the gates: filthy, ragged, emaciated, with long, tangled hair and beards and nails like talons, but with a piercing hatred in their eyes. Scipio chose 50 of them to be set on one side for his triumphal procession in Rome; the rest were sold into slavery. Numantia was demolished and, as in

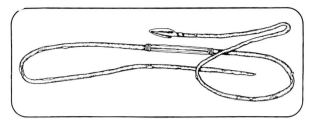

A *soliferrum* as it was found, ritually bent or 'slighted' after the death of its owner—a custom found in several parts of the ancient world. These spears, completely of iron, were 2m long; some examples have silver inlay decoration. (Author's drawing)

the cases of Carthage and Corinth, its reconstruction was forbidden. A cavalry unit was permanently garrisoned in the area to prevent the re-occupation of the ruins. Numantia fell at the end of July or the beginning of August 133 BC, after a nine-month siege; but since no booty was left for the Romans, Scipio had to pay the bonus of seven silver *denarii* to each of his soldiers out of his own pocket. He received his triumph, in 132 BC, and was honoured with the additional title of 'Numantinus'.

The fall of Numantia was not the end of Hispanic resistance; many other cities, for instance Termantia, continued to hold out for many years. It took the presence of an emperor to solve Rome's problems in Hispania once and for all. It was not until after the campaigns of Augustus, in 19 BC, that the last focus of resistance in the Iberian Peninsula was snuffed out.

Armour and Weapons

The body protection used by Hispanic warriors was basically similar to that of other peoples of the ancient world, but evidently showing some local characteristics. The head was protected by a helmet of some kind, varying from a simple leather cap to more elaborate examples, of mixed construction or entirely of metal, with e.g. a triple crest (Strabo) or a zoomorphic decoration of some kind. Unfortunately, this deduction comes to us solely on the authority of ancient chronicles and surviving vase paintings, sculptures and coins: to date, archaeology has provided no single, unmistakable example of such a helmet. Fragments have been tentatively identified, but could also come from bronze or iron pots. One explanation for this lack of

For comparative purposes, a *falcata* **sabre, and a straight Hispanic sword with 'atrophied antennae' pommel—the overall length is comparable, and the blade shape of the latter reminds us very clearly of the later Roman adoption of this admired weapon. Between the two swords are a medium-sized spearhead, and the typical and widely used anular bronze** *fibula* **brooch-pin of ancient Spain. (Necropolis of Valdeganga, Albacete)**

primary evidence could be that these helmets were made of perishable materials—believable in the case of the poor warrior, but hard to reconcile with the variety and complexity of the types indicated, however crudely, in the vase paintings.

Ancient historians made a clear distinction between two types of Hispanic infantry: the *scutati* or heavy and the *caetrati* or light, the reference being to two types of shield. The *scutati* carried the classic long *scutum* of Celtic origin, and probably distinguishable from those carried by more northern peoples only in the matter of decoration; the *caetrati* carried the *caetra*, a Latin corruption of a local name for a small, round buckler. The combination of *caetra* buckler and *falcata* sabre was apparently the most favoured battle equipment among Hispanic warriors. The buckler was made of wood, anything from 30cm to 60cm in diameter, with metal fittings and ornaments on the face, and a large metal boss covering a stout iron handgrip on the inside. Characteristically, it was slung on a long carrying strap when out of battle; in combat the strap might be attached firmly to (wound around?) the forearm. Due to its lightness, the user could both parry enemy blows and also wield the buckler as a secondary weapon, punching for the face or chopping at the arms with the edge.

Body armour seems to have been made from various materials, including simple fabric such as linen, thickly woven panels of esparto grass, hardened leather, and metal plate, scale and mail. There is evidence for the use of round breastplates strapped over fabric or leather cuirasses; the metal plates were sometimes plainly finished, sometimes decorated elaborately in relief with zoomorphic or geometric designs (see Plate A). The use of scale corselets is very clearly indicated on vases; and in some cases there seems to be a suggestion of corselets of mixed scale and mail construction, the scale on the upper torso and the more flexible mail covering the abdomen. There is also a strong indication, particularly on the vase from Liria (Valencia) depicting six riders and six infantrymen, that some horses were armoured with extensive areas of mail. This vase shows foot soldiers wearing mixed scale and mail armour, carrying the heavy infantryman's *scutum*, and armed with spears and the ubiquitous *falcata*. There is also evidence for the use by some warriors of metal greaves.

Spears

In ancient times the spears used by Hispanic warriors were described very variously, and by many different terms; this would perhaps indicate that there was a wide variety of different models in use. Modern archaeological research has permitted some degree of classification, in two main groups: conventional spears with wooden shafts, iron heads and pointed ferrules; and an all-iron type, called by the Romans *soliferrum*.

The conventional spears display a range of head sizes. Examples exist with heads more than 60cm long, enough of these having survived for them to be considered as a distinct class—perhaps used by the heavy *scutati*, though this is guesswork. A second class may be identified by heads in the range of around 20 to 30cm; these may have been carried, several at a time, as javelins by the lighter infantry. Several vase paintings clearly show the use of javelin thongs, wound round the shaft to impart a stabilising spin, and additional thrust, when it was thrown. There are references to Celt-Iberian warriors throwing spears with blazing bundles of grass tied to the heads, not at buildings but in order to break up close-order infantry formations. The conventional spear seems to have been used by foot and mounted warriors alike.

The *soliferrum* varied in length, up to a maximum of around 2 metres. It had a small, barbed head; and was probably a very effective weapon, especially at short range, where its great weight concentrated in the small head permitted it to punch through shield and cuirass and into the body of the victim.

Correlation of some ancient texts with the finding of certain large iron weapon heads, now in the collection of the Archaeological Museum of Zaragoza (Caesar Augusta), allows us to tentatively identify another type of throwing weapon termed a *tragula* or *makhila*. This was a hybrid, something between an axe and a small dart, which was used together with a long leather thong by which it was recovered after a throw. Antique Iberian coins minted for different cities usually bore on the reverse military motifs representing riders armed with different weapons, perhaps suggesting that the warriors of that community were specialists in the use of the weapon represented? Among these weapons is a strange, pointed item which might perhaps represent the mysterious *tragula*; however, the most common weapon shown is a long spear. Axes, though mentioned in some texts, do not appear to have been much favoured in Hispania.

Hispanic Swords
The Romans have passed into history as a pragmatic people who never hesitated to adopt for their own benefit the equipment and practices of the peoples they brought within their empire. The Spanish wars provided a major impetus in the evolution of the Roman army; and contact with the Hispanic warriors forced changes in dress, weapons and tactics. One of the most famous examples was the adoption of the magnificent short sword known thereafter as the *gladius hispaniensis*, the classic legionary sword of the Imperial army.

The swords used by Hispanic warriors fall into two simple classifications: the straight and the curved. The straight type was typical of the Celt-Iberian tribes, and the curved sabre was normally associated with the Iberians; but the picture is

Left, a typical 'warrior pack' comprising a straight sword with two spearheads and a curved knifeblade thrust under the scabbard framing. *Centre*, another 'pack', the sword with typical antennae on the hilt, and a spearhead and curved knife carried on the scabbard. *Right*, a straight sword with another type of hilt. All these finds came from the necropolis of Almedinilla, Cordoba; in spite of the fact that Almedinilla is in Iberian territory, these weapons are in fact more typical of the Celt-Iberian tribes of central Spain. (Author's drawing)

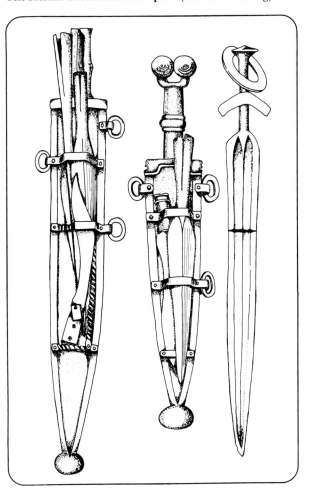

complicated by the fact that examples of both types are found in both cultural regions.

References to the *gladius hispaniensis* in ancient texts are abundant, but confusing. We know that in 225 BC the Romans were using a short sword similar to that used by the Greeks; but, impressed by the superiority of the weapons used by Hispanic mercenaries encountered during the Punic Wars, they decided to adopt them, calling them 'Spanish swords' from this date. Confusingly, both straight and curved types were termed *gladius hispaniensis* at this time; it may be assumed that the Romans adopted both types, but it is obvious from the design which survived into the Imperial era that the straight type found more favour.

It has been possible to identify the prototype of the Celt-Iberian straight sword by making retrospective comparisons between examples excavated at Arcobriga (Monreal de Ariza) which are no later than 300 BC, and 1st century AD finds and sculptural representations of legionary swords. The necropolis finds of Castilla have also added some information. The density of finds of such swords increases in tombs of the 3rd century BC. Essentially they fall into two types. The first, classified as 'atrophied antennae', have iron hilts drawn up into two short 'horns' ending in ball-shaped ornaments. Examples of this type with rich silver and gold inlay decoration are not uncommon. The relatively short blade was sharpened on both edges and had a sharp stabbing point, making it deadly in combat. This sword certainly reached the Peninsula in a primitive form during the Celtic invasions of the 6th century BC, and was later to develop locally in the isolation which followed the Iberian conquest of the south of France in about 500 BC. In vase paintings, and actual finds, it is noticeable that warriors carried knives, extra spearheads, and even scissors slipped under the framing of the sword scabbard.

The second type of straight sword, also in use but much less favoured, was one corresponding to the typical patterns of 'La Tène I and II', of which very few examples have been excavated[1].

The Falcata

This curved sabre was without doubt the favoured weapon of the Iberian warrior over several centuries. Its origin is unknown, but there are two schools of thought: one holds that it was an evolved form of the curved 'Halstatt' knife of central Europe, which had spread to Italy, Greece and Spain, similar types being used by the Etruscans, Greeks and Hispanics. The second theory is that the *falcata* was a direct copy of the Greek *machaera* or *kopis*, brought to Spain by Greek merchants or by the mercenaries recruited by the Greeks around the 6th century BC.

(There is a third theory which holds that this was an indigenous creation; this is not absurd, but the influence of Greek culture throughout the Mediterranean is known to have been so widespread that historians have given little credence to this idea.)

What is known with certainty is that its use and manufacture were perfected in Spain, and the texts are explicit in this respect. The necessary mastery of metalworking did not hold any secrets for the Hispanic craftsmen. In reference to the process of manufacture, Filon writes: '. . . [regarding] the preparation of the above-mentioned iron sheets for the so-called Celtic and Spanish swords: to test if these are good, they take the hilt in the right hand and the point in the left, holding it horizontally above the head, then pull downwards on both ends until they touch the shoulders, then release them quickly. Once the sword is released it straightens again without showing any kind of distortion. This is due to the fact that the iron is extraordinarily pure, and is worked on later with fire, in such a way that it does not contain . . . any defect; neither does the iron get too hard or too soft. After this, they beat it repeatedly when cold, as this gives the iron flexibility. . . . Do not forge it with great hammers, neither beat it with violent blows, because these, if given obliquely, twist and harden the sword throughout its entire thickness in such a way that if we tried to flex it it would not yield, but would break violently due to the compactness of the hardened material. . . . They therefore beat the sheets while cold on both surfaces, hardening each side, while the inner part remains soft from not having received the blows, which reach the depths of the metal only lightly. The sword owes its flexibility to being composed of three layers, two hard and one soft one in the middle.'

We may add some details taken from Diodorus: '. . . The process of manufacture . . . is very special:

[1]See page 70

they bury the sheets of iron, leaving them until rust has destroyed the weak part of the metal, leaving only the more solid part of it. With this iron they produce excellent swords and other weapons of war.' Again, a quotation from Suidas: 'The Celt-Iberians surpass all others in [the matter of] the *machaera*, this has a very useful point and [can deliver] a powerful blow with its edge. For this reason the Romans abandoned their old type of sword after the wars against Hannibal and adopted the Iberian weapon. In reality they adopted the shape, but not the quality of the iron, which they never managed to copy exactly . . .'

In order to corroborate the classical texts, tests were carried out to determine the carbon content of fragments of *falcata* blades found in burials. The results confirmed the high degree of perfection achieved in tempering and cementation. The surface contained carbon to a depth of $\frac{1}{8}$in., the quantity decreasing progressively and no carbon traces being evident in the very centre of the blade. The hardening process had changed the martensite into fealite, confirming the procedure of cementation by burying in addition to the habitual tempering procedure of water cooling and later hammering. The proportions of carbon varied on a harmonic scale and from the wider part of the blade, in such a way that only with difficulty could it be improved by the most modern techniques: the scale was 0.4% in the edges, decreasing through 0.3%, 0.22%, 0.09% and 0.02% to zero.

Written testimony to the effectiveness of this blade survives, as in the case of a veteran legionary of the civil wars in Spain who said, on meeting Caesar: '. . . I am not surprised that you do not recognise me. The last time we met I was fit, but in the battle of Munda I lost an eye and all the bones of my body were crushed. Neither would you recognise my helmet if you could see it, for it was struck by a Hispanic *machaera* . . .' (Seneca, *De Beneficiis*, V, 24).

The peculiar shape of the sword, widening towards the point, moved the centre of gravity further forward than in the straight sword; this increased the kinetic efficiency of a blow. Diodorus comments that these swords were of such quality that no helmet, shield or bones could resist their strokes. Only the inside edge of the *falcata* was sharpened—though it has been possible to confirm

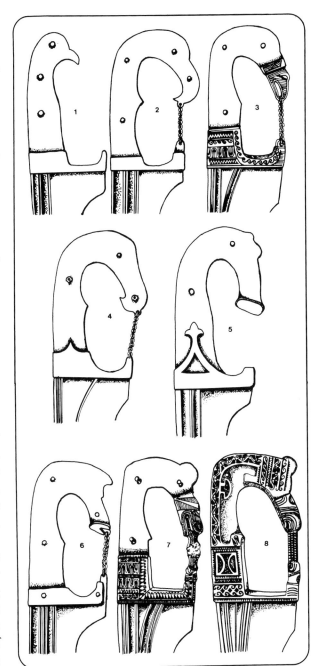

Falcata hilts, illustrating the evolution of this weapon from 'bird's-head' to 'horse's-head' hilt shape, examples of fist protection, and decoration: (1) Tozar, Moclin (Granada), Museo Arqueológico de Granada; (2), (3) and (4) Necropolis of Almedinilla (Cordoba), Museo Arqueológico Nacional, Madrid, nos. 10471, 10481, 10470; (5) Necropolis of Villaricos; (6) and (8) Almedinilla, Museo Arqueológico Nacional, Madrid, nos. 10473, 10475; (7) Necropolis of Illora (Granada), Museo Cerralbo. (Author's drawings)

that some warriors sharpened the back edge at the point. If we accept the evolution of the *falcata* from the Greek *machaera*, we can also make a classification of the different types of hilt, which were often richly decorated with silver inlay.

The older examples, dating from around the 5th and 4th centuries BC, seem copied directly from Greek prototypes, and typically have bird's-head hilt shapes. As the use of this sword became more general the hilt shape changed to resemble a horse's head. Finally, the hilt design degenerated into a purely geometrical and functional shape. The hilt was also fitted with protection for the fingers in the form of small chains or prismatic bars. There exist some examples, of great beauty, which break the classification sequence attempted above, such as that found in the necropolis of Almedinilla (Cordoba) shaped like a bat's head.

As mentioned, the older examples found in the burials of Villaricos can be dated, by means of imported Greek vases found with them, to the 5th and 4th centuries BC. In the 1st century BC, when the propraetor P. Carisius ordered the minting at Emerita Augusta (Mérida) of a silver *denarius* to celebrate his victory over the Cantabri in 22 BC, the conventional representation of the weapons of the vanquished still included the *falcata* and the *caetra*: convincing evidence for the long use of these characteristic Hispanic items.

The size of the *falcata* varied around a mean of about 60cm. The most usual way of carrying it was in a scabbard of leather, wood or fabric with iron reinforcement at the edges, throat and chape. Three or four rings attached to the edges allowed the warrior to sling it on a long baldric from right shoulder to left hip, the sword thus hanging almost horizontal, with the cutting edge at the bottom.

Hispanic Cavalry

The horse enjoyed great importance in the social and military activities of the ancient Hispanics. The horse was honoured as a divinity, and sanctuaries were dedicated to it; an important example has been discovered in Mula (Murcia), which proves very clearly the religious significance of the horse. (It has also provided us with a fine collection of sculptures representing horses with all their fittings.) Another source is provided by the large number of vases decorated with scenes of hunting and warfare found in the ancient village of Liria (Valencia). An additional source is the range of bronze votary figurines found in some Andalusian sanctuaries, usually representing mounted warriors in attitudes of prayer.

The Hispanics made widespread use of cavalry in all their campaigns, not only on Spanish soil but also overseas during mercenary service. A good example of their effectiveness is provided by the campaigns of Hannibal, whose army included large contingents of Spanish horsemen. They not only fulfilled the traditional, rather peripheral rôle of light cavalry as a force to distract the enemy, but also proved capable of defeating in battle the best Roman cavalry when led by able commanders. Poseidonios wrote in praise of Hispanic horse, and considered them superior to the Numidians.

Spain was rich in wild horses, described in many Roman texts as being very fast and of great beauty, while being of moderate size. Strabo and Poseidonios praised their stamina, as they were usually ridden by two men over long distances. The riders used saddle pads of wool, linen or hide secured by a broad leather girth. A recently discovered fragment of painted stucco shows a horseman seated on a mottled feline pelt—presumably that of a lynx, since the leopard was unknown in Spain. Although cloths or pads were the most common, the saddle proper was not unknown in Spain; some vase paintings show them in use, and also spurs, although the stirrup was not used.

During the 4th century BC the Celt-Iberians may

A Hispanic coin from the city of Arsaos, showing a mounted warrior holding a strange weapon shaped like a broad barbed arrowhead; this is thought to be the *tragula* or *makhila*, described in the text. (Author's photograph)

have made an important contribution to the art of warfare by the invention of the horseshoe. Dangerous though it is to make such bold assertions, we can say with confidence that some of the oldest known examples come from central Spanish burials. This invention considerably increased the military potential of cavalry, and influenced the organisation of armies: in Hispanic armies the proportion of horsemen ranged from 20 to 25 per cent of the total force, in the Carthaginian manner, while Roman armies counted no more than around ten to 14 per cent cavalry.

Presumably in a public demonstration of the affection and respect in which they held their horses, Hispanic riders decorated their horse furniture in a liberal, even an exaggerated manner. Among the decorative elements clearly discernible in vase paintings are a small bell hanging from a throat-lash; and a wide variety of prominent frontal

A fine example of a bronze votary figurine from La Bastida de les Alcuses, Valencia. This could depict an Iberian *regulus* or military leader; he holds a *falcata* and, on the far side of the horse, a *caetra*. This shape of helmet, both with and without a crest, seems to have been the most common. The discovery of this piece finally demolished the school of thought which had argued that all Iberian helmets were very simple and uncrested. (Museo Arqueológico de Valencia)

Sculptures depicting horses fully harnessed, datable to the 3rd-2nd centuries BC, from Fuente la Higuera and the sanctuary of El Cigarralejo (Murcia).

ornaments attached to the brow. Many forms, sizes, and (presumably) colours were used, usually based upon a central pivot of metal (iron, bronze, and in the case of noblemen, silver) supporting flower-like crested ornaments of animal hair or coloured vegetable fibre. The neck of the horse was also bedecked in some cases with what are interpreted today as net-like caparisons of coloured wools. Many anthropologists trace a link from these styles right up to our own day, and the traditional decoration of Andalusian horses for festive occasions with rich straps and pendants.

The Iberians had an advanced knowledge of horsemanship, and trained horses and riders with care. One exercise was to train the horse to kneel and remain still and silent on the appropriate signal, a useful skill in the context of the guerrilla warfare which they often pursued. In battle the Hispanic horsemen sometimes played the rôle of 'dragoons', dismounting to fight on foot alongside their hard-pressed infantry in an emergency. On other occasions they formed a ring with the horses in the centre, presumably to protect these valuable creatures from injury. Their mounts apparently had some kind of picket pin attached to the reins, to allow the rider to tether them in battle. The armament of the cavalry does not appear to have differed significantly from that of the foot soldiers, comprising spears and swords; and the *caetra* was the favoured shield, being hung on the side of the horse when not in use.

Balearic Slingers

Among the specialised troops who fought sometimes for, sometimes against the Romans, depending upon the historic circumstances, the slingers of the Balearic isles deserve special mention. These warriors were famous all over the ancient world for their skill in handling their simple but terrible weapons, which were capable of great accuracy, and of crushing metal helmets and cuirasses.

They owed their fame in part to the systematic use made of them by the Carthaginians in all their campaigns, particularly during those against the Greeks in Sicily in the 5th and 4th centuries BC, and those mounted against the Romans by Hannibal in the early 3rd century. At the battle of Zama the slingers, among numerous groups of Hispanic mercenaries, still played an important rôle.

Their skill with the sling was developed from childhood, when they began intensive training at the hands of their fathers. One of the first toys they

A very interesting sculpture, which when found still retained traces of the colours with which it was painted in the 4th or 3rd century BC. It perhaps depicts the richly decorated armour of a warrior of high rank: cf. Plate A. (Museo Archeológico de la Alcudia, Elche)

were given was a sling; it is said that when they began to show familiarity with it, a piece of bread was placed on a stake, and the trainees were not allowed to eat it until they had knocked it to the ground. It is easy to understand the high degree of mastery shown in adulthood by slingers trained by such methods. A little-known detail is that each man used three slings of different lengths and sizes, to throw missiles to short, medium and long range. The sling was carried wound around the brow, as a hair-band. It was made of black rush, animal hair, or animal sinews banded together.

The missiles of small and medium size were made of lead or ceramic material; for the heavier ones, we may presume that any suitable stone picked up on the battlefield would have been used. The lead sling bullets, ellipsoid in shape, were poured in moulds, six or eight together. It is common to find large numbers of these missiles at almost every discovered ancient battlefield, besieged city or other archaeological site in Spain, testimony to the widespread use of the weapon all over the Peninsula and not only in the Balearics.

Common sense suggests that slingers must also have carried a sword and *caetra* for personal protection at hand-to-hand range. In the Balearics some examples have been found of an atypical model of sword which may be defined as a degenerated *falcata*, and which may have been a type used by the slingers.

Considering that the sling was cheap and easy to make and handy to carry, it may have been used as a secondary weapon by spear- and sword-armed warriors. The sling has a long tradition in Spain, and even today it is still in frequent use among the shepherds of Castille and Estremadura, as the author had the opportunity to observe while collecting material for this book. We have confirmation of the effectiveness of the sling from 123 BC, during the conquest of the Balearics by Quinctus Caecilius Metellus. When the Roman fleet was sailing round the islands looking for suitable landing-places, Metellus was obliged to order screens of animal hides to be extended along the sides of the ships to protect the crews from the missiles thrown at them from the shore.

Details of a mounted warrior, and of horse's heads, from 2nd-century vase paintings. The central figure is a horseman from the Liria 'vase of the armoured warriors'; note that the horse is depicted as armoured with, apparently, mail—though the exact arrangement of the leg protection should perhaps not be interpreted too literally? The three heads at left, from various contemporary vases, show bells, frontal ornaments, and neck decorations; at right are three others from the same vase as the central figure, showing different frontal ornaments, but all apparently with mail neck protection. (Author's drawings)

The Plates

A1, 2 & 3: Iberian chieftain, lady, and tribesman; late 3rd/early 2nd century BC

Figure A1 is reconstructed from three sculptural fragments from the same site, and apparently from the same group; like the altar, and the lady, A2, these discoveries were made around ancient Alcudia (Elche), near modern Alicante. The magnificent pectoral or breastplate is a unique find – see photo, p. 138 – as all other representations of breast discs have, at most, simple geometrical decorations. In ancient Spanish mythology the wolf stood for death and disaster; perhaps this motif was chosen to inspire fear? Fortunately, the sculptural fragment retained faint traces of the original pattern and colour, allowing this reconstruction of the tunic. The helmet is of the simple 'bascinet' shape seen in so many of the surviving representations; we cannot know for certain whether it was of bronze, or of leather with metal reinforcement at the edges. (Smiths who could produce work of the quality of the breastplate would have had no difficulty producing any helmet they wished, but the lack of archaeological finds is frustrating.) The altar to which this chief offers up his horse-head

A magnificent sculpture of a warrior fully armoured for combat; note the breastplate of disc shape held in place by broad straps, and the shoulders protected by broad pads of some kind. He holds a *caetra* strapped to his left arm, and a *falcata* in his right hand, unfortunately broken here. He is also armed with a large knife; and the waist sash or band can be seen at his right hip. (Museo Arqueológico de Jaen)

falcata, with a silver and niello-decorated hilt, bears a bull in representation of fertility, and resurrection; and three concentrically carved 'doorways' on the vertical surfaces of the plinth, representing the three 'doorways' of life: childhood, manhood and senility.

The lady, A2, is reconstructed from the sculpture known as *La Dama de Elche*, considered a masterpiece of ancient Spanish art. Ploughed to the surface by a farmer in 1897, it was at first thought to be a fake, and the Spanish government allowed the more astute French archaeologist Pierre Paris to buy it for the Louvre; it was returned, with some other Spanish artefacts, in 1940—partly as a result of Hitler's pressure, at a time when Germany wished to woo Gen. Franco. Originally a complete lifesize figure, the Lady of Elche has been sawn through at the torso; the lower half is reconstructed here from other, contemporary sculptures found at El Cerro de los Santos (Albacete). Remaining traces of colour allow us to reconstruct the appearance of the robes with some confidence. The magnificent headdress is thought to be of gold. The Lady of Elche may be admired today in Madrid's National Archaeological Museum.

The tribesman, A3, wears the standard Hispanic costume: a white linen or woollen tunic, and a cloak of rectangular shape folded over in the manner shown and fastened at the shoulder with an anular fibula. Note that the head is tonsured, a known fashion among the ancient Spaniards.

B1, 2 & 3: Iberian warriors, late 2nd century BC
These figures are reconstructed from the evidence provided by the ceramic bowl from Liria (Valencia) – see photos, pp. 113, 114 and 115. The composite cuirasses shown on the painted vase clearly have scale armour torsos; the lower parts could be of iron or bronze ring mail—or, it has been suggested, could even be meant to represent thickly-woven esparto grass matting, which would be difficult to penetrate. Of all the figures, only one is represented with a crested helmet (B1), and is thus probably a chieftain. We show him carrying a

soliferrum: the vase painting also clearly shows spears, *falcatas*, and classic Celtic *scutum* shields, as B2. There are numerous ancient representations of the kind of 'toothed crest' or comb shown on B2's helmet, which seems to be made of or covered with scale protection—the materials must be conjectural. B1's trophy reminds us that, like many other contemporary European cultures, the Hispanics took heads as trophies of war. B3 is a rider whose horse is armoured with some kind of mail protection and decorated with the characteristic frontal ornament (in coloured wools?); the detail of the horse's leg armour must remain problematic—see photo p. 139.

This group certainly represents an élite type of warrior, from the level of armour and equipment, and possibly they are *auxilia* serving with the Roman armies in Spain. It is also possible that they represent men of the Edetani or Contestani tribes, on geographical grounds.

C1 & 2: Hispanic horsemen, 2nd century BC
C3: Roman citizen cavalryman, 2nd century BC

Our references for C1 and C2 are a mixture of vase paintings and sculptures, and particularly the bronze votary figurines found at La Bastida de les Alcuses (Valencia): one of these shows finally beyond doubt that sweeping helmet crests were not unknown among Hispanic warriors – see p. 137. The ancient writer Strabo described Hispanics wearing helmets with three crests, and there are also references to iron helmet-masks rather in the manner of those worn by the Romans for their cavalry sports; but for the moment we have no archaeological evidence. Note the colourful horse-trappings, apparently in coloured wools or similar materials; the bell hung on a throat-lash is a very common ornament in vase-paintings. C1 wears a round breastplate hung on a strap harness with broader shoulder-pieces, and is armed with the classic *falcata* and *caetra*. C2 wears the simplest type of helmet of all, a leather cap with his own long hair pulled through a hole in the crown. They are fighting a Roman citizen cavalryman from one of the armies sent to Spain during the long wars of the 2nd century. He wears a Boeotian helmet, and a heavy mail shirt with a reinforcing cape at the shoulder; his horse furniture is of Celtic type.

D/E: Hispanic warriors, 2nd century BC

'Somewhere in Hispania Ulterior', a group of warriors from different Hispanic tribes await the right moment to spring an ambush on the Roman column in the valley below . . . Although we have obviously grouped widely differing figures together entirely for our own convenience, it is worth pointing out that large confederations of warriors from several tribes were by no means unknown during the Spanish wars.

D1 is thought to represent a warrior of the Carpetani or Oretani, and is based on a bronze votary figurine. He is armed with several all-iron *soliferrum* javelins; a straight sword with 'atrophied antennae' hilt, and a curved knife stowed on the face of the scabbard; he carries a *caetra*, and wears a characteristic broad, metal-furnished belt. The helmet, as so often, is a problem; it may be of leather with a metal reinforcing band round the brows.

This sculpted warrior's head illustrates the most common form of helmet, a close-fitting 'bascinet' shape with emphasised bands of reinforcement around the edge; there are some examples, like this 3rd-century piece, which seem to indicate crest ornaments in animal shapes—broken here. (Museo Arqueológico de Jaen)

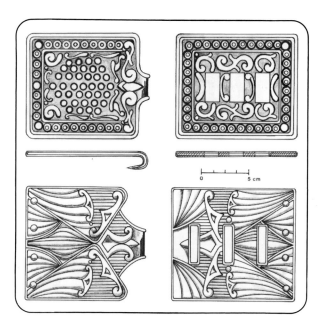

Two examples of two-piece belt buckles, both richly inlaid with silver; the originals are in the Museo Arqueológico de Alicante. (Author's drawing)

This style of tunic decoration seems to have been popular over a long period.

E2, also from a votary bronze, is interesting in that he wears a crested helmet, and what appears to be a hardened leather cuirass under his bronze pectoral disc. Under his broad belt is worn a coloured sash or band whose fringed or slit end hangs down on his right side. The significance of the frequently depicted feature is not clear; it seems more typical of the Baetic tribes, and may have indicated tribe or status by its colour? This man is possibly from the Turdetani or Oretani.

E3 represents a Lusitan warrior. His richly-inlaid straight sword, again with a knife and/or spear-heads stowed under the scabbard frame, is based on one now in the museum of Alcocer do Sal at Belem, Portugal, but similar examples have been found in other parts of the central Peninsula. The round shield, with an iron boss covering the handgrip, is a good deal larger than the *caetra*; its decoration comes from a vase-painting. His spear has a throwing thong looped around the point of balance. The exact significance of the strapping harness round his torso is not known; something like it appears in several votary figurines. Before battle, some long-haired warriors like this man tied their hair behind the neck; others gathered it in a net—cf.

Plates F2, H1; still others gathered it in a pad on top of the skull, for extra protection.

Figure E4 is based on the well-known funerary sculpture from Osuna (Sevilla) showing two warriors fighting; the strange headgear has defied all efforts at interpretation, though very clearly depicted in the sculpture—there have been attempts to associate it with Strabo's description of 'caps of sinew', but this is only guesswork. His other features—the short tunic with coloured edging and a cross-over effect at the neck, his spined Celtic *scutum*, and his horse-headed *falcata*—are all typical.

If E4 is difficult to interpret, D5 is still more so. He is based on a vase-painting of a group of warriors; and apparently wears a caped hood—presumably of leather—with a comb or toothed crest of the same material. Note the very long fringing on his tunic, and the torso strapping, again of unknown purpose. Note also the angled foot or ferrule of his spear, taken from an archaeological find. E6 reminds us that the Hispanics trained their horses to kneel down and remain silent in order not to betray hidden warriors.

F1: Andalusian warrior, 2nd century BC
F2, 3: Balearic slingers, 2nd century BC
F1, based on a bronze votary figurine found in an Andalusian sanctuary, is thought from his hair-style and some other details to show influences from other Mediterranean cultures—perhaps he represents a man who had served as a mercenary for the Greeks? The tunic drawn down to a central point at the front was characteristic of an older style; and note, too, the intriguing quilted finish—for warmth,

Two horns, made of ceramic material and thought to be war-bugles, found at Numantia; while the plain type on the right is the most common sort found, the wolf's-head example is particularly interesting: we should recall that the wolf was the symbol of death. (Author's drawing)

or protection? The tunic neck may have had the same cross-over effect as E4.

F2 and F3 are slingers from the Balearics, as described in the text; they wear simple tunics and minimal equipment. One ties his hair back with one of his three slings (three were normally carried, for different ranges); the other prefers a hair-net. F2 has a long knife, characteristic of finds in the Balearics, which faintly recalls the *falcata* shape. Both figures are based on literary descriptions and archaeological evidence.

G: Celt-Iberian warriors, c. 150 BC

An impression of what Numantine warriors may have looked like at the time of their successful repulse of Nobilior. G1, perhaps fighting as a mercenary or ally a little north of his home range, is based on a sculpture found at Porcuna (Jaen). Note the hanging sash-end or slit band, similar to that worn by E2; the 'bascinet' helmet, this time with a hair crest; the typical breastplate harness, worn here over a heavy garment of leather, or perhaps sheepskin; and the triangular dagger. G2 is blowing a ceramic horn, of which more than 50 examples have been found at Numantia—strongly suggesting some practical function, such as military signalling. Note two characteristic features: the long, heavy cloak of the dark brown wool of local sheep, and the *caetra* hanging low on a long sling. This strap was tied or wound firmly round the forearm before entering battle. G3 wears basically similar kit to G1; but note the checkered tunic hem, and the helmet—from a vase-painting—with a boar's-head crest which appears to be extended into a plume-holder. Note, again, the tonsured man in the background—this style was by now out of date, but probably still seen among older men.

H: Celt-Iberian warriors, c. 130 BC

We imagine here one of the desperate attacks on the Roman walls of circumvallation carried out late in the final siege of Numantia by the starving defenders. H1, who has just thrown a *soliferrum* with a bundle of burning grass attached, has his hair caught up behind the neck in a net. He wears a caped mail shirt—either a Celtic style, from one of the northern tribes, or a captured Roman example: at this date our sculptural evidence shows them to have been very similar. H2 and H3 are our attempts to interpret two very stylised but obviously carefully detailed warrior figures from a painted vase found at Numantia. H2 wears, perhaps over a leather hood giving some protection to the cheeks and neck, a conical helmet of Montefortino type, with a plume. These have been found in some numbers in northern Spain, and a similar one was discovered in the necropolis of Las Pedreras (Huesca). H3 seems to have a 'bascinet' helmet with three (feather?) frontal plumes, and raised rivet or nailhead details. His fringed tunic is decorated with what may tentatively be interpreted as woollen balls or pompons. Both men wear trousers, and bronze greaves. Both have the usual broad, metal-furnished belts, and long La Tène swords.

While not clear in this photograph, the paintings of two warriors on this Numantine vase do yield some clues as to local war-costume, and we draw upon some tentative interpretations for Plate H. The left hand man appears to wear a tall helmet with a long plume or crest, over some kind of hood-like headgear. The right hand warrior has the more common 'bascinet' shape of helmet, perhaps with standing feather plumes; he is armed with a straight sword and a buckler, and behind him are shown two javelins fitted with throwing-thongs. Both men have very slim waists emphasised by broad belts with metal fittings; and both are clearly shown to wear greaves. (Museo Numantino, Soria)

COMPANION SERIES FROM OSPREY

CAMPAIGN

Concise, authoritative accounts of history's decisive military encounters. Each 96-page book contains over 90 illustrations including maps, orders of battle, colour plates, and three-dimensional battle maps.

WARRIOR

Definitive analysis of the appearance, weapons, equipment, tactics, character and conditions of service of the individual fighting man throughout history. Each 64-page book includes full-colour uniform studies in close detail, and sectional artwork of the soldier's equipment.

NEW VANGUARD

Comprehensive histories of the design, development and operational use of the world's armoured vehicles and artillery. Each 48-page book contains eight pages of full-colour artwork including a detailed cutaway.

ORDER OF BATTLE

The most detailed information ever published on the units which fought history's great battles. Each 96-page book contains comprehensive organisation diagrams supported by ultra-detailed colour maps. Each title also includes a large fold-out base map.

ELITE

Detailed information on the organisation, appearance and fighting record of the world's most famous military bodies. This series of 64-page books, each containing some 50 photographs and diagrams and 12 full-colour plates, will broaden in scope to cover personalities, significant military techniques, and other aspects of the history of warfare which demand a comprehensive illustrated treatment.

AIRCRAFT OF THE ACES

Focuses exclusively on the elite pilots of major air campaigns, and includes unique interviews with surviving aces sourced specifically for each volume. Each 96-page volume contains up to 40 specially commissioned artworks, unit listings, new scale plans and the best archival photography available.

COMBAT AIRCRAFT

Technical information from the world's leading aviation writers on the century's most significant military aircraft. Each 96-page volume contains up to 40 specially commissioned artworks, unit listings, new scale plans and the best archival photography available.